An Orange Tree Theatre production

LITTL
JESU

G000269714

by Arinzé Kene
Directed by Tristan Fynn-Aiduenu
Winner of the JMK Award 2019

Cast
Kehinde **ANYEBE GODWIN**
Joanne **RACHEL NWOKORO**
Rugrat **KHAI SHAW**

Direction **TRISTAN FYNN-AIDUENU**
Design **TARA USHER**
Lighting **BETHANY GUPWELL**
Sound **NICOLA CHANG**
Movement Consultant **DK FASHOLA**
Casting **NADINE RENNIE CDG & SARAH MURRAY**

Production Manager **LISA HOOD**
Production Technician **RHEA JACQUES**
Company Stage Manager **JENNY SKIVENS**
Deputy Stage Manager **HELEN COBB**
Technical Assistant Stage Manager **RHEA JACQUES**
Associate Sound **JOHNNY EDWARDS**
Production Electrician **CHRIS McDONNELL**

Thanks to Roehampton University production department

This production opened at the Orange Tree Theatre on
18 October 2019

ANYEBE GODWIN
Kehinde

Anyebe Godwin trained at Rose Bruford College.

Theatre includes: *Jekyll and Hyde* (UK Tour, Touring Consortium & Rose Theatre Kingston); *Manifesto* (Oval House); *Namibia Nao! UK* (Stonecrabs/Soho Theatre); *Four Minutes Twelve Seconds* (Trafalgar Studios/Hampstead Theatre); Serious Heroes (Old Vic New Voices) and Pandora's Box (UK Tour/Spora Stories).

TV includes: *Dreaming Whilst Black, Autopsy: Last Hours of Notorious B.I.G., Doctors* and *The Evermoor Chronicles*.

RACHEL NWOKORO
Joanne

Rachel trained at Arts Educational Schools, from where she graduated in September 2019.

She was part of the Roundhouse Poetry Collective 2016-17 and the Roundhouse Resident Artist 2017-18. She was also UK Poetry Slam Champion in 2016. Rachel's debut poetry collection, *Little You*, was published in May 2019.

TV includes *It's A Funny Old Week* with Jason Manford and *Genie in The House*.

Her work as a director includes *Funeral Flowers* (The Bunker Theatre, Free Word Centre, Bernie Grant Arts Centre).

Rachel can be found on Twitter and Instagram: @RachelShapes

KHAI SHAW
Rugrat

Khai Shaw trained at Rose Bruford College, from where he has just graduated.

Theatre includes: *Decades* (Ovalhouse); *Joe's Birthday Party* (Old Red Lion); *The Railway Children* (Waterloo Railway Theatre); *Daddy Cool: The Musical* (Shaftesbury Theatre); *The Lion King* (Disney); and *Chitty Chitty Bang Bang* (London Palladium).

TV includes *Meet the Adebanjos, Casualty and The Complete Guide to Parenting. Landmark Productions, The Bryan Quinn Theatre Company, Spotlight Productions, C21 Theatre Company* and *HotForTheatre*.

Director Tristan Fynn-Aiduenu and Anyebe Godwin in rehearsals for *Little Baby Jesus*

TRISTAN FYNN-AIDUENU
Director

Tristan Fynn-Aiduenu is a British-Ghanaian writer & director hailing from South London. He has studied at Roehampton University & Royal Central School of Speech & Drama.

Directing Credits include: *Timbuktu* (Theatre Royal Stratford East); *Sweet Like Chocolate Boy* (Jack Studio & National Tour); *Black Attack* (Bush Theatre); and *Beyond The Canon Showcase 2018* (RADA).

TARA USHER
Designer

Tara is a London based Set and Costume Designer, trained at Wimbledon College of Art and now working across musical, dance and drama productions.

Most recent productions include: *Queen of the Mist* (Charing Cross Theatre); *Heart of Darkness* (The Marlowe Theatre); *A Midsummer Night's Dream* (UK Tour, Immersion Theatre); *The Barber of Seville* (UK Tour with Surrey Opera); *Queen of the Mist* (Brockley Jack);Nuns (Tristan Bates Theatre); *Sweet Like Chocolate Boy* (Brockley Jack and UK Tour); *See Me For Myself* (Tabard Theatre); *Treasure Island* (Trinity Theatre); *Sweeney Todd* (The Minack Theatre) and Rising Festival (The Roundhouse).

Further examples of Tara's work can be found at: www.tarausherdesign.co.uk

BETHANY GUPWELL
Lighting

Bethany Gupwell studied Lighting Design at The Royal Central School of Speech and Drama. Bethany was the recipient of the Association of Lighting Designers Francis Reid Award 2018.

Lighting Design credits include: *I'd Rather Go Blind* (Omnibus Theatre); *Trade* (2019 Tour); *Queen of The Mist* (Charing Cross Theatre); *Wonder Winterland* (Soho Theatre); *Keep Watching* (New Diorama); *Bobby & Amy* (Vaults Festival 2019); *Zorba* (Performance Preparation Academy); *Immersive Dining Experience: The Great Christmas Feast* (The Ugly Duck); *Sweet Like Chocolate, Boy* (Brockley Jack); *Caucasian Chalk Circle* (Royal Central); *#Dr@cula* (Leicester Curve) and *Free* (Royal Central).

Associate and Re-lighting credits include: *The Rite of Spring – Seeta Patel* (2019 Tour); *Black Men Walking* (Bernie Grants Art Centre); *The Phlebotomist* (Hampstead Theatre); *Seussical* (Southwark Playhouse); *Dust* (Trafalgar Studios); *Heartbreak House* (Union Theatre) and *Carmen* (Union Theatre).

Assistant roles include: *Come from Away* (Phoenix Theatre); *Beginners* (Unicorn Theatre), Lighting Intern on *Hamilton* (Victoria Palace Theatre); *Beacons* (Park Theatre) and *Natives* (Southwark Playhouse).

NICOLA CHANG
Sound

Nicola is a composer/sound designer for theatre, film and commercial media across the UK, US and Asia. As a performer, she currently plays for *Six* (West End) as Dep Keys/Musical Director and she is a former cast member of *STOMP!* (West End/World Tour). She is also an Artistic Associate of the King's Head Theatre and a BFI x BAFTA Crew Member.

She has performed at the Royal Albert Hall, the Royal Festival Hall and the Shakespeare's Globe as a percussionist, and holds a MMus in Composition from King's College London. Additionally, she is a Composer and Musical Director attached to British Youth Music Theatre UK.

Her theatre credits include: *The Tempest* (Orange Tree Theatre); *The Ice Cream Boys* (Jermyn Street Theatre); *Wild Goose Dreams* (Theatre Royal Bath); *The King of Hell's Palace* (Hampstead Theatre); *The Death of Ophelia* (Sam Wanamaker Playhouse, Shakespeare's Globe); *Summer Rolls* (Park Theatre); White Pearl (Royal Court); *From Shore to Shore* (Manchester Royal Exchange/UK Tour); *Lord of the Flies* (Greenwich Theatre); *Dangerous Giant Animals* (Tristan Bates Theatre); *Finishing the Picture* (Finborough Theatre); *A Hundred Words for Snow* (Arcola Theatre), and *The Free9 (*National Theatre).

Anyebe Godwin and Rachel Nwokoro in rehearsals for *Little Baby Jesus*

DK FASHOLA
Movement Consultant

DK Fashola, is an Actress and Multidisciplinary Artist who specialises in multi-form storytelling; fusing movement, witty dialogue and poetic multi-layered text in unexpected ways.

DK is the Artistic Director of Initiative.dkf (2019/20 Tamasha Associates) and Creator of Melanin Box Festival and Scalped. She's also a 30 Nigeria House Award Winning Artist with Theatre Royal Stratford East and 2012/13 Royal Court Young Writers Program Alumnus.

Movement credits include: Movement Director and Creator of *Scalped* (UK Tour / Without Walls); Movement Consult and Assistant Director of *Hotel Cerise* (Theatre Royal Stratford East) and Movement Coach on *Becoming* (R&D, The Albany and Stratford Circus)

Choreography credits include: Dis Luv Music Video (Wizkid, Tiwa Savage and Dj Spinall); Assistant Choreographer for Davido Concert (O2 Arena).

Notable theatre credits as an actor include: *Mami Wata - WIP* (Bush Theatre); *Ile La Wa* (Stratford Circus) and *Muscovado* (UK Tour - Winner of the 2015 Alfred Fagon Audience Award)

Playwright credits include: Theatre 503 (2018), VAULT Festival (2017) and RADA Festival (2015).

Other Credits include: Assistant Director on *Hatch* (Talawa Theatre/ Hackney Showrooms).

NADINE RENNIE CDG
Casting Consultant

Nadine was in-house Casting Director at Soho Theatre for fifteen years; working on new plays by writers including Dennis Kelly, Bryony Lavery, Arinzé Kene, Philip Ridley, Laura Wade and Vicky Jones.

Since going freelance in January 2019 Nadine has worked for Arcola Theatre (*HOARD; The Glass Menagerie*), Leeds Playhouse (*There Are No Beginnings*), Sheffield Crucible (*The Last King of Scotland*), Fuel Theatre (*The Little Prince*) and continues to cast for Soho Theatre.

TV work includes: BAFTA-winning CBBC series *Dixi*, casting the first three series.

Nadine also has a long-running association as Casting Director for Synergy Theatre Project and is a member of the Casting Directors Guild.

Khai Shaw in rehearsals for *Little Baby Jesus*
Photos by Ali Wright

JENNY SKIVENS
Company Stage Manager

Jenny recently became Company Stage Manager for the Orange Tree Theatre for the 2019/2020 season. She also stage manages dance and choir events for City Academy

Orange Tree Theatre credits include: Directors Festival 2019, *Merchant of Venice, Romeo & Juliet, Poison* and *King Lear*. Other theatre includes: *Our Town* (Regents Park Open Air Theatre); The Unknown Island, Dear Elizabeth (Gate Theatre); *The Wolves* (Theatre Royal Stratford East); *We Know Not What We May Be* (METIS); *Othello, Julius Caesar* (Guildford Shakespeare Company); *Alice in Wonderland, ShelfLife* (Volcano Theatre Company); *The Radicalisation of Bradley Manning* (National Theatre Wales); *World Enough & Time* (Fluff Productions); *A Suicide Note From Palestine* (Freedom Theatre), *Jack & the Beanstalk* (Polka Dot Pantomimes); *Golgotha* (Conspirators' Kitchen); *R3* (Centre Five Productions); *Sense & Sensibility* (Rosemary Branch Theatre/Yvonne Arnaud); *Cinderella, Merchant of Venice, Antony & Cleopatra, Tales From King James, Doctor Faustus, Rapunzel or the Magic Pig, Romeo & Juliet* (Creation Theatre Company)

Other credits include: *The People's Tower* (Birmingham Hippodrome); Proms at St Judes Music & Literary Festival and Commonwealth Games Handover Ceremony (Birmingham Hippodrome); Machynlleth Comedy Festival and *City of the Unexpected* (National Theatre Wales), Open East Festival (Barbican Centre) and SummerSalt Festival (Melbourne Recital Centre).

Crew credits include: Barbican Concert Hall, BBCSO and LSO

HELEN COBB
Deputy Stage Manager

Helen trained at the London Academy of Music and Dramatic Art in Stage Management and Technical Theatre.

Much of Helen's career has been spent touring the UK and internationally with such productions as *Sesame Street Live* (Premier Production); *Dead Sheep* (Cahoots Theatre Company) and *Peppa Pig's Adventure* (Fierylight Productions). Most recent role was as Deputy Stage Manager on *The Glass Menagerie* at Watford Palace Theatre and the Arcola Theatre.

RHEA JACQUES
Technical Assistant Stage Manager

Rhea has worked in technical theatre and stage management since graduating from Rose Bruford College in 2017. Since May 2019 Rhea has been Production Technician at the Orange Tree Theatre. During 2018, Rhea was Resident Technician at Greenwich Theatre, and Interim Technical Instructor at Rose Bruford College. Rhea also assists with set building and carpentry.

Her credits at the Orange Tree Theatre include: *Amsterdam,* Directors Festival 2019, *The Tempest* and *While the Sun Shines*.

JMK trust

in memory of James Menzies-Kitchin

The JMK Award was established in memory of James Menzies-Kitchin, who staged his first production in 1994. In the following year and a half, he established himself as a theatre director of thrilling promise. He was committed to staging classical theatre of the highest quality and was an entrepreneur of unstoppable drive. His clarity of vision, his tenacity of purpose and above all his courage, inspired all those who worked with him. In 1996, at the age of only 28 James died suddenly and the Trust was set up to encourage others to fulfill their potential, as he had promised to do.

The JMK Trust was founded to give opportunities to young theatre directors of similar ability and vision. The JMK Award allows one such director a year to stage their own production of their chosen text.

Recent winners include:

Josh Roche 2017, *My Name is Rachel Corrie* by Katharine Viner & Alan Rickman

Roy Alexander Weise 2016, *The Mountaintop* by Katori Hall

Liz Stevenson 2015 *Barbarians* by Barrie Keeffe, nominated for an Olivier Award for Outstanding Achievement at an Affiliate Theatre

Kate Hewitt 2014 *Far Away* by Caryl Churchill

Alex Brown 2013 *The Island* by Athol Fugard, John Kani & Winston Ntshona

Sam Pritchard 2012, *Fireface* by Marius von Mayenburg

Cathal Cleary 2011, *Disco Pigs* by Enda Walsh

Past winners include Natalie Abrahami, Caroline Steinbeis, Joe Hill-Gibbins, Polly Findlay and Bijan Sheibani.

'The Award is extraordinary because its unique existence fulfills every young director's wish: to choose a play and then receive the financial support to stage it. It was an amazing privilege to have this wish fulfilled.' Natalie Abrahami, winner 2005

The JMK Award 2019 is kindly supported by Philip Hooker, the Martin Bowley Charitable Trust, the Directors Charitable Trust, the Backstage Trust, the Fidelio Trust, the Leche Trust and all our individual donors.

Registered Charity No. 295080
www.facebook.com/jmktrust   Follow us on Twitter **@JMKTrust1**
Find out more about us at **www.jmktrust.org**

ORANGE TREE THEATRE

A powerhouse of independent theatre

The Orange Tree (OT) is an award-winning, independent theatre. Recognised as a powerhouse that creates high-quality productions of new and rediscovered plays, we entertain 70,000 people across the UK every year.

The OT's home in Richmond, South West London, is an intimate theatre with the audience seated all around the stage: watching a performance here is truly a unique experience.

We believe in the power of dramatic stories to entertain, thrill and challenge us; plays that enrich our lives by enhancing our understanding of ourselves and each other.

As a registered charity (266128) sitting at the heart of its community, we work with 10,000 people in Richmond and beyond through participatory theatre projects for people of all ages and abilities.

The Orange Tree Theatre's mission is to enable audiences to experience the next generation of theatre talent, experiment with ground-breaking new drama and explore the plays from the past that inspire the theatre-makers of the present. To find out how you can help us to do that you can visit **orangetreetheatre.co.uk/discover**

orangetreetheatre.co.uk

Registered charity no. 266128

REAL TALK

Foreword by **Tobi Kyeremateng**

*Dem man would say dem man are mandem and us man are dem man
But then my mandem would say us man are mandem and dem man
are dem man.*

Kareem Parkins-Brown, *Sunny D or The Purple Stuff?*

Optional reading soundtrack: *'Sittin' Here'* or *'Do It'* by Dizzee Rascal
(Boy In Da Corner, 2003)

Since the early 2000s, I have seen the language of my ends archived
in the mouths of the teenaged youth of the third millennium and
evolved through cultures, shifted by the latter end of Generation Z.
In my school, mandem recited 'P's and Q's' like a Sunday prayer
with not a single syllable missed, and some of South London's most
loyal playground ambassadors would later join in reciting 'Talkin'
Da Hardest' with the same religious inflection, honouring the joining
of North, South, East and West through this National Anthem of the
ends. In a new decade, the mandem of the 2010s would forge their
own worship here. The language of my ends has always sat between
an electric poem backed against the pacey riddim of an old-school
grime track, and the war-cry that escapes when the first noticeable
seconds of our favourite tune drops in a dance. So much of the
beauty of theatre exists in the subtexts we give language to; the
private jokes only specific cultures could dictate, the space between
the beat and the silence which speaks emotions 'proper' English
doesn't have words for, and the fact that 'fam' has approximately 10
different meanings depending on how we say it.

This language allows us to preserve our own histories in our personal
archives, and this oral tradition has historically given communities
that have been oppressed permission to keep these histories
relevant and authentic. The stories I grew up hearing Kano and
Dizzee Rascal spit through the speakers of a Sony Ericsson Walkman
W810 sit comfortably in my archive alongside the stories the likes of
Arinzé Kene, Bola Agbaje and debbie tucker green have dedicated
to our stages. The stories we tell ourselves about the cultures we
consume can help us question the presentation of the theatrical self,
and characters like Kehinde, Joanne and Rugrat in *Little Baby Jesus*
not only taught me about the compelling and complex personalities I
was raised around, but emphasised the power of language moulded
by inner-city ecosystems. The friendship between Obi, Myles and
Cain in *Estate Walls* is reminiscent of the boyhood-to-manhood I

witnessed with my peers in similar settings. Watching a show and being able to say, 'I know that character personally', 'that character right there is my aunty-who-isn't-actually-my-aunty', 'boy, that used to be me once upon a time' is a privilege not everyone has, and when it comes around, it is glorious.

'Come like Cyclops Polyphemus the way he be watching me.' (Joanne, *Little Baby Jesus*) – The beginning of a sentence starting with 'Come like' already lets you know a madness is about to follow, and it'll most likely be all types of funny, extra yet true. Young people from ends have always had a knack for pulling from the wildest references to deliver a very specific yet subtle description of feeling, and in this case, it's the glare from an infamous Greek monster.

'You make me happy like when the Oyster machine on the bus ain't working.' (Chelsea, *Estate Walls*) – Only a few of us will be able to relate to the pleasure of a free bus ride once adulthood punched us square in the face in the form of having to part with our money and hand it over to TfL. The wave from the bus driver moving you along to the seats as the Oyster machine rang red felt like an 'I got you' directly from God, saving you that extra coin you'd later spend on something frivolous and joyful.

There's a sophistication to the way we speak that hasn't always been welcome in our theatres and our society despite Black, working-class cultures being a key synergist of homegrown British entertainment, and for some this rejection is internalised in the politics behind 'speaking proper English' and dubbing this syntax as 'Ghetto Grammar' to dismiss the validity of building community-led languages in a society that teaches us that expression is only valid through the gaze of white acceptance. Poor young people and those adjacent to them are consistently villainised by what they wear, what they eat and how they speak by people that believe culture and/or Blackness is monolithic.

Performing respectability is a much-loved theatrical piece of the colonial gaze which has pockets of communities that have been oppressed running away from our salvation, but respectability can never be our saving grace when its very birth is symptomatic of white supremacy, and art cannot operate in a vacuum when these dynamics of power exist in every space we occupy. Our internalised -isms are reproduced in the ways in which we watch and respond to the work we see, and if we truly believe in the future development, diversity and accessibility of theatre, we must ask ourselves the necessary question of how we as individuals are helping keep the languages of our city alive and away from endangerment.

From Patois to Nigerian Pidgin, slang and abbreviations, the ends carry an assurance and culturally rich palette that lets me know I am home, and this feeling isn't all too dissimilar from the poetics of a nostalgic grime track or the first ever play you saw that truly represented the whole of you.

To my young g's from ends:

The multilinguists; the performers; the code-switchers; the mandem and gyaldem; the gang gang gang; the makers and thinkers; the playground hustlers; the back-of-the-bus caretakers; the street poets; the riddim creators and adlib instigators; the multifaceted culture pioneers of our London city streets - your lingual legacy is something to be preserved and upheld. Speak up and speak tall; speak boldly and daringly.

Gwaan wid yuh bad self. Real talk.

LITTLE BABY JESUS

Characters

RUGRAT, *ex-schoolboy*

JOANNE, *ex-schoolgirl*

KEHINDE, *the boy who never leaves*

Synopsis

A lyrical triptych of monologues based around the lives of three distinct school pupils. Each account is a riveting narrative relaying the exact point that a teenager becomes an adult. They are written to be appreciated together.

Set in contemporary inner-city London.

This text went to press before the end of rehearsals and so may differ slightly from the play as performed.

PROLOGUE

KEHINDE. As the world gets better at spinning.

JOANNE. We get dizzy and fall on our rare.

RUGRAT. Some keep falling through the atmosphere.

KEHINDE. Some don't survive past 12:05.

JOANNE. But if you've got *this* – (*Heart.*)

RUGRAT. And if you use *this* – (*Brains.*)

KEHINDE. Then you don't need much or a little bit else.

ONE

Kehinde

(KEHINDE *is sixteen, black. He is mature, very sensible for his age, but there is a sensitivity about him; an innocence.*)

I used to have 'mixed-raced-girl syndrome'. Mixed-race-girl syndrome is the long obsessive phase of over-fancying mixed-race girls. Girls of that lighter complexion. Most guys get it when they're like fourteen, fifteen. My favourite was when that black African or Caribbean skin mixes with that white English or European skin. You get that sun-kissed finish.

At one point. I actually wanted to be mixed-race. I wished for it. I wished my hair wouldn't curl over itself like pepper grains, I wanted it to be bouncy and coolie. But no, broom bristles instead I concluded I was stuck with. I'd gladly have traded this nose for one that was sharper at the end. Shameful, I know. I was so stupid, I got down one time, asked God to forgive me for my sins, to protect my family and to bless me with pink lips. I actually remember going to sleep wishing that I'd wake up with green eyes.

My prayers were obviously ignored and I didn't turn into a mixed-raced boy. And if I were God I would've blanked me for a year just to chastise me for being so ungrateful of this beautiful black skin I was gifted with – Praise God. Believe I had a lot of growing up to do.

Well, I couldn't have grown up all that quick though because next I got a really light-skinned girlfriend. I just couldn't leave the lighties alone. Said, if I couldn't be one, I'd have to represent one – to compensate.

My grandma calls it 'Yellow Fever'. She said it all started around slavery times when white overseers would secretly admire the beauty. I'm sure that back then it was nothing to rape black women. Africa was like the white man's back garden and he did whatever he saw fit with his fruit. She said it's not our fault though, she says something's wrong with us. She always used to say –

(*Nigerian accent.*) *'You African men are magnet for oyinbo pehpeh too much. You de follow-follow and think you are among dem but they will let you know how black you are. IF you trust a white man to build the ceiling above your head, you mustn't complain of neck problems, my child, na your fault be dat!'*

If I bring home a girl who's any bit lighter than me then –

'Ah-Kehinde! It's getting late, your oyinbo friend has to go home. Doesn't she have a home or have her parents split up?'

Cos all white people's parents are divorced according to Grandma.

My older brother, he would sneak girls into the house all the time. When Grandma would go by his room, he'd get the girl to hide down on the side of the bed, on the floor.

Joanne's Prelude

(JOANNE *is a schoolgirl, fifteen years young, mixed-raced, fresh-faced, dipped in rudeness and rolled in attitude. She wears her school uniform and a pink mini-backpack. She is only young but something about her is profoundly jaded. She is a lot older than her years.*

She stops to stick her chewing gum under a desk.)

JOANNE. When you're born
      You should get
      A manual that says:
      'Okay listen up, you have seventy-five years to be all you
      can be!'

CHORUS. GO!!!!

JOANNE. Rather than wastin' your time, getting caught up with
      things like... religion.

CHORUS. And finance.

JOANNE. And school!

CHORUS. Schooooool!

JOANNE. Flippin' school.

CHORUS. Schooooool dinners.

JOANNE. Oh! Don't EVEN get me started on da food.

CHORUS. It ain't soul food.

JOANNE. And it ain't food for thought.

      It gets all stuck between your cheek and your gums AND it
      slides down your throat too damn slow. No joke. This one
      time, the fucking chips took so long to get to my belly that I
      thought I was gonna choke. Could not breathe. It stopped in
      the middle of my chest and just jammed there. Had to take

three mighty swigs of *IRN-BRU* to wash it down. Oil-drinking simulation. Real talk – next lunchtime I'm boppin' straight out of school gates for a smoke and that's me. I beg a teacher try chat dust to me about smoking in my uniform and see if I don't tiger-punch a dinner lady through her temple to send her staggering for pavement – Real.

But what's worst than school. After school I haunt the 271 bus route for a couple journeys to kill time before I touch the morbidity that is a place I'm forced to call my home. Don't even wanna put my keys in the door more-times but that's the only door I got keys to. Ptshh. It's Mum, innit.

CHORUS. Mum Mum.

JOANNE. Can I switch the telly on?

CHORUS. Mum Mum.

JOANNE. But Mum, I can't sleep.

CHORUS. Mum Mum.

JOANNE. Mum, I'm not being funny…

CHORUS. Mum Mum.

JOANNE…. but can I have my dinner money please?

CHORUS. Mum Mum.

JOANNE. Aaaahh MUM!

CHORUS. Mum Mum.

JOANNE. You're so… you're so dumb!

CHORUS. Mum Mum.

JOANNE. You make me wanna die.

CHORUS. Mum Mum.

JOANNE. THAT'S WHY I'LL NEVER BE A MUM!

I will throw my baby away before she goes through anything you put me through.

(JOANNE, *on her journey to school, 'rocks' (customises) her school uniform.*

*She rolls up the skirt until it is too short. She pulls her
popsocks up to the knee. Fixes her hair bun to one side.
Buttons down her school shirt to show a bit of cleavage, and
turns the shirt collar out.)*

Joanne

Whenever we had science and we'd do lessons on magnetism,
by the end of the lesson there'd always be a few magnets
missing. At least one of them were in *my* pocket. It's a known
fact that human beings love magnets. No matter how old you
get you still find them fascinating.

When I was younger, primary-school days, I'd carry around
this magnet that I'd stolen from school and on my journey
home I'd see how many things it was attracted to. It killed me
doing that. I'd stick it on the railings, on gates, on the postbox,
drains, lamp posts, doorknobs, cars, telephone box, bus stop,
fences. I think people are like magnets. When we come
together we repel or attract.

Me and my mum are red magnets, so we repelled. Constantly
trying to get away from each other. We hated being out together.
Like... I had to go hospital one time cos I slipped in the shower.
See, most people sing in the shower. I dance. That's how I got
this scar. Slipped and split my head open on a tile. I remember
that day like it was Monday. The water in the shower turned
pink all of a sudden. It didn't hurt until I saw blood.

Had to wait for-eh-ver at A&E. Just me and Mum, in public,
uuh, nuff uncomfortable. Nuff people who came after us were
getting seen to first. That was making Mum vexed. On some
Incredible Hulk flex – anger problems. She's one of those
people, once she gets started, everything, Every Little Thing,
pisses her off. So she's sitting in her chair at one hundred
degrees Fahrenheit – just fuming. She kept telling me to close
my leg –

'Close your leg, girl!'

It's really not that big a deal. I sit with 'em open, so what?
We're not in the 1800's – real talk. If I'm wearing jeans I wanna
feel free to go – (*Opens legs.*) ya get me? I'm there finking –

*'Mum, Mum, I broke my fucking head tonight yeah and you're
obsessing over my open leg. Please. I beg. Get over yourself.
It's not that deep.'*

Didn't actually say that to her though, she would've blasted
another gash up-side my head – real talk.

We got back home and I think she was still upset –

'Joanne, go and wash your blood out the shower curtain.'

She was so nice to me sometimes?

Rugrat's Prelude

(RUGRAT *is a class clown, underachiever, shit-stirrer,
playground loudmouth. He's on the outer of the inner circle.
Hanging with the bad boys but always watching, and
commentating, never getting his hands dirty.*

RUGRAT, *in lunchbreak detention, is indignantly writing lines.
He keeps looking out of the window –*)

RUGRAT. I must not disrupt this class
    I must not disrupt this class
    I must not disrupt this class
    I must not disrupt this class

    Ah dis is long! (*Shortcut.*)

    I I I I I I I

    Must Must Must Must Must Must Must

    (CHORUS *join in.*)

    Not Not Not Not Not Not Not

    Disrupt Disrupt Disrupt Disrupt

This This This This

Class Class Class Class Class Class Class Class Class Class
Class Class

CHORUS. Sometimes

CHORUS. I'm doing it

RUGRAT. Just so you can notice me

CHORUS. Notice me, notice, just so you can notice me –
(*Repeat over and over.*)

RUGRAT (*talking to Mr Taruvangadum, over the* CHORUS).
Oi, sir. Sir! Can I go now?
I'm finished though, look.
Everyone else is outside playing football.
Sir!
But other people were saying it too, why didn't you say
nothing to *them*?
OH MY DAYS! How was it only me though? Jerome!
Jerome said it before me even. Yeah, you *wouldn't* hear him,
would you. You've got selective hearing you know that, sir?
Nah nothing, I said nothing.

(*Flops back down in his chair, crosses his arms.*)

THIS IS SO UNFAIR!

(*Under his breath.*) Ah shut up, man, look at your head.
…Pardon?
Yeah… (*To himself.*) but you never say anything good about
me though, do you? Never say *I* got a bright future ahead of
me.
(*Mumbles.*) Please.
I *said* please!
Thank you.

(RUGRAT *jumps to his feet and races out of the classroom…*

*…reaching the playground just as the ball is blasted over the
fence. Disappointed.*)

Rugrat

Ahh! I flipping hated whenever the ball went over the fence.
And you know who toe-punted it, innit? Babatunde. That guy,
man. When he first come to our school in Year 9, this is no lie –
on his first day he was wearing sandals, blood. Sandals. Man
was like –

'Where you going with those, rude boi?'

Teacher was bussing up, he tried to keep a straight face but it
was the way he just sidestepped into registration; firstly, no one
knows who he is, secondly, man had SANDALS. (*Laughing*.)

I was dead, I died – ah Jerome, Jerome's my boi, innit, Jerome
said something like how –

'Babatunde got those sandals from Jerusalem, rude boi!'

Wooo! That is what sent me. I flung my chair across the room, I
was cry-laughing, rolling on the floor and all sorts –

'Did you rob them sandals off Jesus, fam?'

'That's why Jesus had no shoes on the crucifix.'

Every cuss! He-Got-It. Babatunde.

He was bare strong though. No one believed he was in Year 10.
He was probably in Year 10 about ten years ago. Hench,
muscles on top of muscles. And he had these long arms that
dropped below he's knees – borderline orang-utan.

I swear, we 'attempted' to rush him one time after school – at
the bus stop. Jerome went to fling him by his rucksack. Blood.
He just, blood, Babatunde just turn't around and did one
fucking... I dunno, it looked sick, he just flung his arm and
Jerome went flying into the bus lane – I thought it was gonna be
some *Final Destination* moment cos the bus proper almost hit
him. Driver slammed the brakes.

Proper close.

Babatunde was blatantly the strongest in our year AND in Year 11 but because he was fresh, he didn't care, he just wanted to get an education. Thing is about my school, certain playboys won't let you get an education without you passing your foundation in street wisdom. Ya gotz ta be streetwise.

Anyway, it was that day in the summertime when all the flying ants start being everywhere. It was interrupting the football and like I said Babatunde TOE-PUNTS the ball over the fence with his size fourteen Oxfam trainer. But what happened next shocked everyone...

(*Pause.*)

He said... (*Shakes his head.*) couldn't believe this.

He said he wasn't getting it!

EVERYONE KNOWS THAT WHOEVER KICKS THE BALL OVER THE FENCE HAS TO CLIMB OVER AND GET IT – simple playground regulations.

He says he ain't getting it – not just that, but the school bell rings, which puts the ball in the position of possibly never being retrieved again! Obviously some passer-by will see that ball, take that ball and make that ball their ball. And it was a good ball too.

Babatunde puts on his blazer and heads out of the playground. Everyone's like –

'Oooh...Liberties!!'

He was taking the PI double. And Terence Cunningham, who the football belonged to, he'd be the last one to go fetch the ball, he got his pride, a reputation to sustain. Terence Cunningham is one of the younger Cali Road Boys, CRB – (*Does the gang hand-sign, fingers forming the letters C, R and B.*) He's older brother, Pierre Cunningham, used to go our school and he was hard as nails. They still whisper his name in the corridors.

'BABATUNDE!!' Terence said.

Baba stopped and turned to face his enemy. Terence Cunningham opens his arms out wide, like wings – (*Demonstrates.*) Animals normally do that as a trick to appear bigger in order to ward off their opponent –

'Is that how it's gonna be?' said Terence.

Then Babatunde just took off his blazer, flung it on the floor hard! The earth shook –

'DO YOU WANT TO FIGHT ME TOO?! EVERY DAY NA THE SAME, SOMEBODY NEW IS WANTING TO FIGHT BABA. MAKE HE NO FIGHT ME-OH! If you fight me your face go be roforofo face, your body go be roforofo body! I done tell him before, make 'e no fight'e'o!'

(*Pause*.)

If I'm totally honest, I think… I might've shitted my pants a little bit when he said that. He was some Nigerian gangster! He laid it on the line! His voice echoed through the playground like a lion's roar through the plains of the Serengeti. *Blood clot*. He had that fire that you only see in the eyes of grown men.

We all looked over to Terence Cunningham. Terence?

Now, there's only ONE THING Terence Cunningham can say that could top *Baba*-tunde's display of sheer *Baba*-rity. And it comes in the form of two words. Nope, It's not 'fuck you' or 'fuck off!' or 'ya mum'. Nah.

It is another set of words that outside of a school means almost nothing.

Terence stood there. Just nodding his head – his face bearing no emotion. Then the two words we were all pregnant to hear rolled off of his tongue and out of his mouth and into our ears –

'3:30.'

Everyone heard that?!?!!

'3:30, blooOOOOood! FIGHT FIGHT FIGHT FIGHT FIGHT FIGHT!'

We went ballistic! I took off my school tie, wrapped it around my fist like a boxing glove and started punching the air. (*Demonstrates*.)

'Fight Fight Fight Fight Fight.'

(*Extremely excited*.) Free-Fur-E.

3:30.

That was IT! Are you mad? Are you unwell? Are you under anaesthesia, fam? We were hyped up, man! We had only fifth and sixth period left – so without further ado, we do what we do best: add fuel to the fire –

'Who'd you think is gonna win?'

'I heard Terence's dad bought him that football for a hundred and seventy-five pound!'

'I bet you Terence's brother comes down!'

'Who, Pierre Cunningham??'

'Baba's gonna get strawberry jam dripping out of his nose.'

'I bet you this – I bet you that.'

'Where's it gonna be?'

Dumb question – errr. About *'where's it gonna be'* – blatantly it's gonna be in the underpass. That's where all the school fights happen...

Kehinde

The day my brother brought this white girl back it was as if Grandma just knew, like she had some sixth sense or something. As soon as she come through the door, she puts the shopping bags down on the kitchen table, where I was watching TV. Normally she'd start packing the food into the fridge, I'd automatically stand up to boil the water for the vegetables before she had a chance to tell me how lazy I was, but no, not today. She marched straight up the stairs and made a beeline to my brother's room – didn't even take off her jacket. Most days, she'd just stand in his doorway and ask him why he weren't doing his homework or why he only vacuumed downstairs but today she must've smelt the sex-funk or something. She went all the way into his room. Shut the door behind her. When I heard that door click shut I had to crack a smile though, cos my brother was always getting away with things. I went and sat on the stairs, didn't wanna miss a sniffle.

White girl is hiding, behind the curtains. Grandma notices the pair of UGG boots sticking out from the bottom. My brother is sat at his desk, with his eyes on a page apparently halfway through some novel. Fooling nobody – he doesn't read. Grandma walks straight over to the curtain and punches it. The curtain screams. She punches it a bag of times. A barrage of punches later and the drapes fall down. She spat in the face of a little white girl somewhere between fourteen and sixteen years old and then gave her the beating of her life.

When she was done she sat on the corner of my brother's bed – sweating, breathing heavily. She had folds of pink skin under her fingernail from when she'd scratched the girl's eyelids. She beat that white girl bad. She beat that white girl like she was the white woman who my granddad cheated on her with. She beat that white girl like she was the white bus driver who closed the doors in her face after she ran all that way to catch it. She beat that white girl like she was the white man in the market who gave her ten pounds' change when she remembers giving him the twenty-pound note that she *just* got from the bank. She beat that white girl the way she would've loved to beat the white woman in customs who made her throw away all the food she had in her hand luggage.

Grandma had a heart condition, so when the white police came to arrest her, the white paramedics came too. She felt that white people had taken everything away from her. So as they were putting her in handcuffs and she was calling them devils and Lucifers and demons, obviously they thought she was crazy. But I knew she wasn't crazy. She wasn't crazy she was just hurt. And conditioned. And that's how she'd be until the perishing day because it's hard trying to tell old people new things when they're stuck in 1974.

My uncle came over to our house that evening and you know what he said to me? He said –

'Kehinde, you are her trophy child, you know that? She has looked after you since you had no teeth so you have to look after her until her teeth fall out.'

Family are so shifty. They are always trying to pass on the responsibility.

Joanne

So we lived in the last house on my road. The only house without a blue door. Mum wouldn't let the council paint it, even though it was free. She believed the Government were fitting cameras in the peepholes.

When I think of that house yeah, all I can think of is 'brownness' because everything was so dry 'n' dusty 'n' old 'n' boring 'n' grey 'n'.

It smelt like mold 'n' medicine 'n' vomit 'n' musty bed sheets 'n'.

The curtains were slow death 'n' Mum kept them closed in the daytime, even. Quite depressing.

That's why me and my magnets were in no hurry returning from school.

Blue door, blue door, blue door, black door.

One time, I open the black door and mum was sitting there. Just sitting there, on the stairs. Right on the middle step. Staring into space. (*Looking behind her.*)

'Muuum?' (*Waves her hand in Mum's face.*)

She had soil in her hands. All up in her fingernails. Up to her wrist. Like she had been digging hard. Or gardening with no gloves. She didn't even acknowledge me – real talk. I follow the soiled carpet. I remember standing over the random hole in my garden, looking in it. Nothing. Just wondering why I couldn't speak with my mum, I started praying?

Rugrat

(*Talking over the same words at the end of* JOANNE*'s speech*.)
I started praying.

Praying that some fool wouldn't blab his mouth to a teacher
about the fight. See, most teachers in this school are pussies in
real life who probably got bullied when *they* were in school, so
when they get an opportunity like this, to stop a school fight,
they leap at it, makes 'em feel bigger. It gives 'em 'staffroom
bragging rights'. Then this teacher would take that velocity, go
off to their lesson and bully some Year 10 who has difficulty
understanding algebraic expressions. Or threaten me with
detention or something – when I *am* trying. I am.

Terence Cunningham yeah, he is hands down the fastest in the
school. One hundred metres, two hundred metres, run for da bus,
race you to the next lamp post, anything, bruv – no one beats
him. He'll even give you a head start. There was no shame in
losing a race to him cos he is a speed demon. When he runs, he
kicks out his leg and produces these huge strides that cover land,
but all that was wasted on the pitch, he's just a goal-hanger.

He got in this fight with a Year 11 when we were in Year 9!
BLOOOOOD – sickest fight. One of the sickest fights. All I'm
saying is, you know when someone gets fly-kicked in their back
and their head proper swings backwards. I remember that in
slow motion. Terence Cunningham can definitely fight.

I wanted Barbaric-tunde to batter him though. Terence was out
of order sometimes, man, him and the rest of the CRB
Youngers. Take that same day yeah, he asked for a DROP of my
Fanta Fruit Twist, a drop. I gives him the bottle now – firstly, he
proper wraps his fish-lips around it (and I ain't drinking it after
that, I might as well kiss him on the lips directly, ya get me, it's
the same ting). Secondly, he boxed it back, all of my drink! In
one go, like it was a drinking contest, then tries to hand me the
bottle back, talking about –

'Dash that in the bin for me.'

(*Kisses his teeth.*)

And then he burped in my face – for no reason. I wanted
Babatunde to do that arm thing to him –

'Guys, can you quiet down!'

It's sixth period now. Pure jokes, it's only RE, Mr Taruvangadum.
He's my form tutor as well so I'm on a hype ting.

'But, sir, look at your head.'

'Jamie, I'm gonna kick you out!'

'Yeah I know but look at your urgent head though.'

'Get your gear and get out!!'

'But your head is oblong though, sir, I'm just saying it's long,
innit, what, I can't say your head is long?'

'OUT!!!'

'Geez, forget this class anyway.'

I walked down the hallway looking in the windows of all the
other classrooms. Everyone's got their heads down – pens
squiggling.

Ya know it feels so good at the time, getting kicked out, but when
you're in the hallway on your Jacks-Jones, you feel lonely like.

I go down the spiral stairs, walking sideways with my back to
the wall in case a teacher looks down from the top and sees me.

I go in the toilets and put my hand behind the radiator. I found a
Nokia-3210 in there once, so now I always check.

I cruise the school like a ghost. Permanent-ink marker in my
hand. I write my nickname:

(*Writing.*) Rugrat. Rugrat. Rugrat.

This. School. Is… Shit.

If. You. Are. Looking. At. This.

You. Are… Officially…

Gay. Married.

Yours. Truly…

Rugrat.

Then I hear a whisper –

'Rugrat.'

'Ah?'

'Your mum.'

'Who's dat, you tramp?'

'I'm your mum, blood.'

'Jerome, you bitch.'

'Ah how'd you know it was me?'

Jerome sticks his head over the top of the cubicle. Anything to show off that he's one of the few boys in my year who have grown a moustache.

'Cos I smelt your breath.'

I check my phone, 3:20.

'Oi, melon head, it's 3:20. So we gotta kill… (*Does the maths on his fingers.*) ten minutes.'

Wanted to go back to RE with Jerome to show Mr Taruvangadum that by throwing me out he only put me with my bredrin –

'Yo. Jerome. What you doing in there anyway?'

'Ah?'

'You floating your logs? Ah? You dropping the kids off at the pool? Oi?'

I prop myself up to look into his cubicle but just before my eyes can focus he puts his hand in my face and pushes my head out. I fell back onto my bum and my permanent marker slid under the sink.

Jerome fiddles around for a bit in the cubicle then swings open the door with his bag slung on one shoulder. Smiles.

'Who's gonna win?'

We walk.

Jerome blatantly wanted Terence Cunningham to win, they were both CRB Youngers, innit.

We walk out the school gates.

Walk down the hill.

We go shop.

I bought a Fanta Fruit Twist – I drank it before Jerome could ask me for some.

We get to the entrance of the underpass and wait.

Before I look at my watch I almost pee myself with adrenalin, in my mind I estimate 3:32. They're probably piling down the stairs by now, pouring out the school gates.

I look at my watch.

'3:20??? I swear we've been waiting for ages.'

'I know.'

Time moves extra-slow when you're waiting for a fight.

3:22. The bus 271 goes by. I look up and you would die if I tell you who was cosy on the upper deck of this bus.

'Oi, Jerome… bruv, is that Babatunde?'

'Babatunde, where you going?'

Jerome grabbed a pebble, small like a raisin and colourful – he dashes it. It bounces off the back window.

When the mob rolled out of those gates it got E-motional. Some next uproar. Me and Jerome held court at the bus stop – had to clap my phone against the red bench for order in the court.

'Ooorder!'

I took the stand and gave testimony about how straight Babatunde's neck was – pretending he didn't see us, begging his own eyes not to wander. By show of hand it was voted that Babatunde deserved to catch a beat-down tomorrow at lunchtime for committing playground statutory offense 22: false almshouse promotion. But before we all boarded our separate buses, Jerome was dying to show us something. He casually unzipped the front bit of his rucksack and held it open for us to see. I looked in the bag. The thing stood upright. I was at the back of everyone but I saw the thing shimmer as it reflected the sun.

Jerome, man.

I think most of us were all suddenly quite glad Baba had caught that bus.

Come the next day we cussed him but we didn't even feel to rush him any more. To be real, I was quite pleased to see him.

TWO

Kehinde

I remember. I spent the whole first day of secondary school trying to find my twin sister, Taiwo. They put us in different form groups and different classes. Looked for her everywhere. Even when I got home she wasn't there. Strolls through the door an hour and a half later without her school tie. And she had the phattest grin on her face. She didn't miss me a little bit. She loved it that we got split up. I hated it. See *that's* when I got the light-skin girlfriend; Rachel. But Rachel wasn't half as smart as Taiwo. And she couldn't draw a circle like Taiwo. My sister could draw a perfect freehand circle like no one in this universe. She'd draw circles in my palm with her finger and I'd close my eyes because it felt nice. She was just good at everything. And she could hold her breath underwater for the longest – longer than anybody I know. Rachel, on the other hand, she couldn't even swim. She wasn't even pretty but she was mixed-raced so people were like –

'Ah saw Kehinde wit dis MIXED-RACED TING, she's buff, man.'

She weren't even buff. She weren't that pretty. Not like Taiwo, my sister is pretty. You can tell straight away she's pretty. She has small eyes and big lips and small teeth. And she has this big mole in her eyebrow.

I couldn't speak to Rachel about anything really. When I got fed up of kissing and fingering her I'd just start thinking about Taiwo, start wondering what she was up to. If it was after school then she was probably playing football. Rachel's dad worked for the council and he supported the school team so even he knows how good my sister is playing midfield. Rachel's dad genuinely liked me –

'You're a golden opportunity, Kehindy,' he'd say.

He was nice, even though he pronounce my name as Kehindy. Kehinde. But he was the first white man that I felt comfortable around, so I didn't correct him.

Rugrat

Four mornings out of five I'm late for school, guaranteed. I mean, they're lucky I even showed up to that ramshackle of a school anyway. When I'm really late, I see a whole group of different faces on the bus. Like this one girl, Jodie. She is so ridiculously buff? It's ridiculous. Gimme heartburn, that girl. She rocks the burgundy uniform cos she goes to EGA Sixth Form. That stands for Elizabeth Garrett Anderson but for us EGA stands for Every Girl Available. No one believes me but I kissed her one time, Jodie.

Swear down – on my mum's life. Before I even started secondary school.

'Twas the summer holiday before Year 7. Who do I see riding her bike through my area? Jodie, the queen of buffness. Courage from within took surface and I told her to stop and then I told her I wanna kiss her round the corner, so she walked her bike round the corner, where I was waiting patiently.

When we kissed her name was Joanne – and she was bless. But school made her remix it to Jodie; her evil side. *Joanne* was nice though. I had my hands on her cold thighs and everything.

When my washing machine broke down I got to see her at the launderette. She used to gel her hair down to her forehead – and it would come down to the side like this – (*Demonstrates*.) Fuck me though, was Jodie rude? That girl was roo-oode! Rude! No one could tell her nothing, boi. She didn't even have to touch you, she'll just drop you one line that'll feel like a t'ump in da face.

One time she roasted this woman on the bus for no reason. No reason! In front of everyone. The woman, all the woman did was ask Jodie politely, to put out her cigarette –

'Who the fuck are you with your penguin shoes, don't chat to me with your breath smelling like wet ass-crack… rah rah rah.'

Motormouth Jodie.

I was pissed when she started going out with Baker. Baker ya know. She had her pick of anyone in the world and she chooses him? He was the dumbest guy in our year. No one will ever truly know how dumb this guy was unless they was in our year. He came out with stupid shit, every single day – of his life. He had dumbness on tap. After a while it just stopped being funny cos, I mean, how can someone be so consistently dumb? Jodie went with him of all people, virginity and everything. Bareback – no protection. Watch Baker come into school the next day walking sideways, talking about his leg is hurting –

'She banged me, bruv, she banged me.'

I was P I doubled. I would've banged her properly. Cos thing is, if you know Baker you know he would've just lied there.

Bitch.

Still love her though.

Joanne

Kristina was this Lithuanian girl who I worked with at the launderette. She had really really bad teeth. What made it worst, she was young. Her breath never used to smell or nothing, her teeth were just bad that's all. She was really pretty when she smiled like this – (*Demonstrates a closed-mouth smile.*)

The launderette was a flippin' electrical mess. Why was the ceiling leaking tumble-dryer water onto the wires for the washing machines? One dirty hazard cycle.

DeathTrap.com, forwardslash, OneDaySomeCustomerGonna-
CatchTheirElectrocutionUpInThisBitchAndSueForAMillion-
Pound – Straight – Real Talk. Nuff people got electric shock
from just leaning on the dryer, ya know. Or from opening the
machine door.

One time, this woman put her carpet in the washing machine. It
washed it yeah, but when it was time for it to come out it wasn't
having it. It was stuck. The water must've made it inflate or
something because initially it was kinda easy to put it in but
pulling it out was the longest.

Me and Kristina tried everything, we were sweating. Was kinda
fun though. When things like that happen at work it's exciting.

The lady whose carpet it was stood out in the street waving down
random guys to come and help us. Like, three different men came
and tried but it wouldn't budge. Then this boy come. He was
kinda skinny compared to the men who had tried and failed. He
had his headphones in and everything, like it was gonna be a
breeze. Anyway he tries for like half a minute then says –

'I'll be back.'

Me and Kristina kinda giggled cos now he's looking kinda cute
in his bright white vest with his skinny self looking all
undernourished. Real talk. And when he said –

'I'll be back.'

his voice was staggeringly deep and freaky like –

'I'll be back.'

(*Giggles, flirting.*) *'Okay, we ain't going nowhere.'*

He left his iPod and his T-shirt on the bench.

The radio behind the till was one of them radios that stay fuzzy,
always stuck in between stations, so I thought I'd listen to his
iPod instead. The tunes were all right still. Skinny boy's got a
little taste.

He comes back. Erm. Why did he bring with him about ten boys
from the estate? They all rode up on their bikes – Myles, Cain,
Obi, Jacob… even my half-brother come but he doesn't speak

to me anyway so… Reuben, Kwame, Rommell, Andrew, Harry, Omar, Hassan, Ibrahim – all of the older lot. Left their bikes spread out on the pavement, making it hard for people to walk past. It wasn't a big launderette but they all squeezed in to try this carpet –

'I bet you any money I'm the one that gets it out, fam.'

They made it a competition. It caused one massive scene, people from other shops were trying to peek in to see what the big crowd was about.

One by one, they tried, pulling at this carpet from different angles. It was like Excaliburs, sword in the stone.

When they got tired of that, they started chatting up Kristina, dropping game on her –

'How comes I ain't never beheld your buffness round here before?'

But when they saw the brown bits on her teeth they all backed off and started cussing each other for chatting to her –

'You're the one that spoke to her, blood, you wanna lips her teeth.'

I felt for her a bit, man – real talk, cos sometimes customers would be like talking about her teeth, blatant, in the shop like she wasn't there. Anyway, all the boys from the estate clear out and ride off on their bikes. Skinny-iPod boy, stays.

Kehinde

I'm in Year 9 at school.

There was this group of boys. The Cali Road Boys. 'CRB' – (*Demonstrates using the hand signs*.) All of them were white, but they made exceptions for *certain* black boys. Like, if you truly supported Arsenal you were allowed in or… if your dad did all kinds of madness that the white boys' dads knew about – things like that. I got sent out of class once but that weren't enough to qualify for the CRB, they only recruited bad breeds. Boys who never bring a pen into school.

A few of them played in the football team. The leader of the CRB was our team striker, his name was Pierre Cunningham. Pierre Cunningham reckoned he could run faster than my sister, and one day during PE he actually said it out loud. Everyone laughed at him of course. Taiwo was *fffast*, the fastest in our year. And she had a really quick start, *zing,* that's how she'd stay ahead the whole race. When she's racing, she should wear a T-shirt with the number '2' on the back so that whoever is behind her knows where they're coming. Second. She is always ahead of whoever is coming second.

After school, the race, was on.

It was, whoever makes it to the fourth lamp pole first, wins.

'On your marks get set GOOO!'

Pierre went early, he had a false start. Everyone saw he ran before we said 'go', he was ahead, but that was cool, no worries, Taiwo was catching up quick. She ran with her back straight, by this time Pierre had already started to swing his shoulders, his form was all messy; means he's tired. When he runs he kicks his foot out so he gets these big strides – an advantage but not a threat. Taiwo had smaller strides but she has good technique, her back, straight – you could iron your clothes on it. Her arms, cutting through the air, *zing-zing-zing,* her feet, moving so swift they barely touched the ground, *zing-zing-zing.* They're neck and neck. They whizz past the launderette at the same time. Pierre's steps were getting heavier and heavier, he was running his hardest, his cheeks were wobbling, but look at Taiwo, the image of composure. Then after they passed the third lamp pole, *ZING-ZING-ZING – Wow.* My sister was holding back all that time. She was only toying with him, she had a LOT left in the reserve... the way she crucified that last twenty metres, boy. Should've seen Pierre Cunningham's face drop. She ran so fast that her shadow had to catch up. He crossed the lamp post a couple seconds later and put his hands on his knees Straight Away.

Taiwo was already at the fifth lamp post, the momentum, cos she was going so fast, the momentum carried her to flipping...

the next hemisphere; she had to walk back. Victory walk. (*Watching her walking back.*) Just cool, not out of breath or nothing, didn't even break a sweat, didn't even complain about Pierre's false start or about the random bikes blocking the pavement, just smiling, grinning them small teeth. Then her smile turned into furrowed eyebrows.

(*A boy in crowd.*) *'Yeah! What did I tell you? I knew Pierre was gonna win! He's t-too fast, no no no, he's th-th-three fast, no no no, he's f-f-f-four fast!'*

Some people were saying that Pierre won!

Joanne

Cute-skinny-iPod-boy gives it one last try. He takes his boney arm that looks like the letter 'L', sticks it in the machine, feels about a bit, turns to carpet lady –

'Did you fold it before you put it in?'

He asks –

'One of the corners are trapped.'

He puts his arm in deeper, and *pop,* the corner come out.

Facile.

Then with two fingers he pulls the whole carpet out. So easily. It was like magic.

Carpet lady was grateful, she started dancing and all sorts, like it was some nuff expensive carpet. Calling him Aladdin, saying that the magic carpet wouldn't move for anyone but Aladdin. I was laughing cos now he kinda looks like Aladdin. Aladdin's skinny, innit.

Don't think carpet lady didn't slip and fall on her backside when she was dancing around! I was cracking up – Real Talk. Cos true she was kinda big, carpet lady. Skinny boy was trying to avoid my eye contact because he would've started cracking too. He helped her to her feet now, but erm… why was her breast blatantly hanging out her bra?

I was like –

'Oi, carpet lady, you're indecent, innit. Your titty, is swinging.'

(*Gestures to pull up bra.*)

Boy. I dunno.

I offered to dry her carpet for free.

She said she didn't wanna risk it.

I do not blame her. Could be another episode.

Hear this, she wouldn't let cute skinny boy leave until she let her reward him with an ice cream from the off-licence next door. Hilarious. Like he was some little boy. That killed me.

He came over and mouthed something to me but I had his headphones in. I handed him back his iPod just as I finished listening to this exclusive Slum Village song that I hadn't heard before, the chorus ended up stuck in my head for days afterwards.

(*She sings a few lines from the chorus of 'Climax (Girl Shit)' by Slum Village.*)

He offered me his ice cream. So sweet –

'Sorry but I don't like Solero.'

The next week he comes into the launderette with a white-chocolate Magnum ice cream. My favourite. And I didn't even tell him, ya know. Obviously I had to give him my number immediately, no long ting. Sorry but, from time a brudda can just KNOW your favourite ice cream, you gotta take that brudda serious – real talk. And not a day goes by after that that I don't think of him. He said his name was Baker. What kinda name is Baker? I just call him Aladdin.

(*Singing.*) *'Like a dream come true…'*

Kehinde

Pierre?! Nah! Pierre didn't win shit!

They were only saying that because they were afraid of him and the Cali Road Boys. Look at Pierre's face, he knows he lost. He weren't showing off like he does when he gets it in the back of the net. Yo Pierre!! (*Walking up to him.*)

He's taller than me but I made sure I got in his face –

'Why deceive yourself, fam? Why, fam? You lost. Accept it. Digest it. Look, look at this, this is the letter 'L', you should eat it. You should marry it. You earned it. You can't win all the time. CRB? Who… Why would anyone wanna be in your scabby crew? I lost mad respect for you, fam. Epic Fail'

Instead, what really came out was –

'Ah Pierre, gotta give it to you, bro, you're kinda fast, that was close but you won, by an inch though, just an inch, that was close but you won, you had a better start, she should've dipped.'

SHIIIT!

What's wrong with me?

My eyes dart over his shoulder in search of Taiwo. Phew. She was occupied, she didn't clock.

That's when I heard a crow caw from the tree above and… there was *something* about this moment.

You… you know when you're brushing your teeth in the morning and you suddenly remember you had a dream last night and you just kinda freeze up in front of the mirror because you're trying to recall it and you almost had it just now but it slipped away? And you have to let it go, carry on brushing and try to forget about it because you know that the more you try and remember it, the further it's gonna repress itself deep down into your inner psyche? *That* feeling. When I heard the crow caw in the tree it jugged something in the quicksand part of my mind and gave me *that* feeling. I knew there was some kinda lesson to be learnt, I felt as though I were reliving a parable.

A CRB throws his scabby arm over my shoulder.

'Who's the fastest in the year, bruv?'

'Err it used to be Taiwo but now it's Pierre,' I said quickly.

Then the pin dropped. I realised what the muffled fluttering under my subconscious was about. It swung my rationale into the story Mr Taruvangadum taught us earlier that day.

Right before they captured Jesus, when he was chilling with his Apostles, he said to Simon Peter –

'Before the cock crow twice, thou shalt deny me thrice.'

It was obvious. The crow's caw was the cock's first crow. Sounds crazy I know but it was a sign.

Up in the tree, the crow stared directly down at me. I barely understood the omen, when Pierre grabbed me by the strap of my school bag and lead me to the middle –

'… even Kehindickle saw!! Tell 'em what you saw, go on, tell 'em.'

I looked up at the crow. My sister's face shot out to me from the crowd.

'Errr. You… Pierre won. Taiwo should've dipped.'

The crow cawed a harsh final cry then flew from the tree. Taiwo heard. She turns her head in shame.

Shit.

That rendered me horrendous.

I pulled my tongue out of Pierre's bumhole and let it back in my mouth where it should've stayed.

FUCK!

I tried to explain to her that –

*'I swear down, he won by an inch, I'm telling you, from where I
was standing, at the angle from which I saw it, he won by an
inch – plus, the sun was in my eye, you should've dipped.'*

– to obvious no avail. She had no words for me, she wouldn't
even look in my face.

'Oi...'

She zipped open her rucksack, barely listening to my false
apologia, turned and articulated one thing:

'You have SO much to learn.'

That shot me through my bad heart ten times –

Ruptured my spleen,
fractured my ribs,
internal bleeding,
haemorrhages,
blood clot,
cataracts,
brain damage,
heart attack.

Death by double-crossing. My one person in the world. If I
were allowed to have one person in the world, I'd have Taiwo.

As I watch her put her trainers into the carrier bag before she
puts them in her rucksack, I promised myself I would never
shun a *blessing* to gain friends ever again. Right then and there,
I grew up. Inside here – (*Touches his heart.*) And the growing
pains sent a tear rolling down my cheek. I had to pull myself
together, quickly.

Taiwo slung her bag over her shoulder and we began our trek
home.

The loser had to kiss the winner's shoe, so Pierre and his pack
kept howling offences. They even started following us home,
said they'd leave when she kissed his shoe. Taiwo won that
race, fair and square, she was not about to get on her knees to
kiss a loser's shoelaces. She told Pierre that to his face. They
got all sore. They started throwing stones. We just kept walking,
trying to ignore them.

Looking back in hindsight, I should've seized that moment to redeem myself, but I shoulda woulda coulda – at the time I was too cut up inside. Not a blood cell or one scintilla in me was invested in heroics. I kept my head down like a professional coward and I tightened my punani.

'Pussy!'

The stones were flying past us. Some of them were rebounding off of car windows, some of them were small like little tablets – hitting my school bag. One of the mixed-raced CRB had a whole handful of pebbles, ran up to Taiwo and put it down the back of her school shirt. She let him do it. Helped him even by slowing down a little so he could pull his wrist out of her shirt collar more comfortably. They all cheer as if it were some wonderful magic trick what he did. The stones dribbled down the bottom of her untucked shirt and beat the ground with every step she took. Occasionally I'd get one in the back of the head but it didn't hurt that much because I was *blessed* with hair that curls over itself, softening the blow, therefore protecting me from things like sharp stones that otherwise would cut me deep. Besides, they were aiming for my sister.

This had gone on for some time now and I could tell she was getting tired of being strong. She stopped and turned around to say something wise probably. That's how they got her in the face. As soon as it left Pierre's fingers he regretted it. He watched it cut through the air, this one was flying on course. The way he dashed it, sideways like he wanted it to skid-bounce across the lake surface. That one was small like a raisin and colourful like racism. It just missed her eye by about a centimetre, embedding itself underneath her skin. But then on this occasion, contrary to the song, the *second* cut was the deepest. Another CRB pitcher lent in with a right arm. This one pitched like he was a descendant of Babe Ruth. It clipped the side of her head. Sending blood trickling around the shape of her ear, down her neck, onto her school shirt and making CRB scatter like P – I – G – E – O – N – S.

Fled. All but one. Pierre, transfixed with eyes a-glaze. He was sorry. There are many ways you can put the fear of God in a child but when they do bad on their own volition and become stained with guilt from it, well... suffice to say a lesson is learnt.

'Yes, bruv, she bleeds. Just like you.'

I felt like her younger brother sometimes. Taiwo was a lot wiser than me, but by culture, even though I came out second, I'm the older twin.

In my tribe, we name the first-born of twins Taiwo. Which means:

'The first to taste the world.'

The second-born is normally called Kehinde, that's my name, it means:

'The last to come.'

But the reason it's said that I'm older, even though my sister was the first-born, is because Kehinde is the one that *sends* Taiwo out of the womb. Kehinde asks Taiwo to check what the world is like outside and to report back. Taiwo is subsequently born. She then communicates to Kehinde spiritually, through the sound of her cries, she lets him know whether life is going to be one of suffering and running or one that's virtuous and playful. Taiwo's reply determines if Kehinde will be born alive or stillborn. So despite me being born second, I'm still the true elder of the twins because I sent Taiwo on an errand. A prerogative of one's elders in Yoruba-land.

Doctors had to shave her head to sew the stitches – same like they do furry pets. She had the whole school in hysterics the day she came back because she had an eyepatch on one side and a shaved head on the other. Only thing she was missing was a hook for a hand and a parrot for her shoulder. Even Mr Taruvangadum laughed at her and he's the RE teacher!

But she was so cool with that, she let everyone laugh it up, she laughed *with* them. She was sooo cool. And in the playground she still played football, except this time, instead of having some indignant defender in goal, she volunteered to be the goalkeeper.

That match was heavy, I joined in, the sun was out, my heart was pounding properly and I didn't get out of breath, not once. When she headered me the ball, I knew she'd forgiven me. She forgave me like Jesus forgave Simon Peter. I watched her in goal. Her smile was back on. Full beam.

Then Pierre and his crew came, like the cloud that blocks the sun. Pierre grabbed the ball and blasted it over the fence. On purpose. Another bid to get a reaction out of Taiwo. All because he got beat by the black girl – who he was deeply in love with. He should've just forgot about what his boys would think and told her that he loved her.

Joanne

When my mum got sectioned I was given some leaflet about a foster retreat. Leaflet had bright colours on the front and all the children in the picture were happy, smiling, daisy-picking, unisex-shirt-and-dungarees-wearing, bright-eyed, *'I went swimming in the LAKE this morning'* type-of-lifestyle-having-looking children. It was up north somewhere. I was getting kinda sick of London, school, people, nosey neighbours, oh my God, NOSEY! Who haven't got the slightest. Who just assume and make up stories and who don't actually know the real FACTS about my mum, and who may find themselves very knocked out, dazed and amazed, if they chat to me sideways, again – real talk.

I was just very bored of all that shi-*T*. Wanted a change of pace. And I felt like I'd stuck my magnet to everything ferromagnetic. I wanted to experience something different so when I got that leaflet I thought, bless, why not? I'll chill with these perfect-life-having children for a summer up north, might do me some good. Maybe like –

Actually wait... I have to go back and finish my story about the launderette because it got a bit mad. My bad...

Remember the carpet fing? One of the first men who tried to help with the carpet was some Greek-looking guy, thick glasses

– funny accent – grey hair – stomach big, like a pregnant woman, nine months. He was lingering a lot afterwards, around the launderette. Few weeks go by and why do me and Kristina notice he's been following us home every weekend? Nasty. But what was even more fucked up: when he came into the launderette, he'd try chat to me. He'd show up, briefcase in hand and it was like he was speaking in verse, being all lyrical and stuff, saying he wanted to *taste* me, talking so slick you could see the crude oil on his tongue. It was blatantly something that he'd rehearsed in the mirror. I'd just tell him straight no chaser –

'Listen, old man, I'm not in the mood for romancing with some weirdo, ya get me, so don't waste your rotten breath, innit, you'll need it to blow out your hundred and fifty candles at your birthday next year, that's if you're lucky to make it through the night with your slow heartbeat like some kinda reptile, and your deep eye sockets, looking like a skeleton already, walking in here dressed like Inspector Morse with your empty briefcase – just trying to look smart, wearing the same suit that they'll bury you in at your funeral. LISTEN! Next time you roll up in here you better have some garments to wash or I will leave you in a grisly state…'

(*A long kiss of the teeth.*)

You can't leave *any* hope for them people, ya know. About you want to *taste* me, *are you drunk on battery acid? Don't make me vomit, sir.*

Looking at me with his Lucifer eyes.

Had to tell him straight, but Kristina though, Kristina would really chat to him, like really chat to him. Anyway, cut a long story short she started feeling the old boy. A little too much. Did everything he said. Launderette was a sweat box but he made her cover up her arms. Then he made her wear a longer skirt to cover up her legs. And before I left, it was obvious that he started beating her because she was covering up her bruises too. With make-up – real talk. Makes me think, is that what good girls get for having bad teeth?

On my last day at the launderette I got the phattest electric shock from the washing machine. I think it was saying goodbye.

THREE

Joanne

I dunno… the retreat was… alright. But everyone was younger than me, which was kinda disappointing – having no one your age there to chat to.

It looked NOTHING like the flyer. Them dere people who made the flyer are jokers – real talk. I gets there now, all the colours had faded on the building. The children there were looking crustified, dear Lord; crust! I thought I had it bad. One of them looked like she was wearing a potato sack. Another one look like he stole his clothes off of a scarecrow. Caveman couture as well; no shoes. Some people do not have it. It's a sad world, man.

On the first day you could tell who and who were gonna clash. It was like the Big Brother House for Teenage Rejects and Unwanted Infants. Some dramatic kids up in there, boy. Crying like it was first day of school. Little Jack was crying like he sold his cow for some beans and never got the beanstalk – real talk. I told everyone straight –

'Oi oi, listen! I'm the oldest here, innit. So like… yeah… just… just have respect and dat… For me.'

Ah, I flopped it, innit. Like George Bush, I had everyone's attention and flopped severely. You know when you tell everyone to stop, and then everyone actually stops dead like, and they're all just looking at you, and that kinda surprises you because you never thought they would pay you any mind, so you forget what you was gonna say? Real Talk.

(Mocking herself.) *'…just have respect for me and dat.'*

We were *all* fucked up in that place anyhow so I blended in nicely with that intro.

There was this girl, Frankie. I think Frankie's a crack-baby, the most hyperest thirteen-year-old in the world. She already had

this raspy voice and she was always screaming and shouting
and talking (bitching) and laughing or whistling that loud
whistle, the one where you jam up two fingers in your mouth – I
hate when people do that indoors. Why? I beg, it's not
necessary –

*'Okay Frankie, we all know you can do it now, stop showing off
– REAL!'*

And boy was she oversexed. Always chatting wet 'bout some
boy who was banging her doggy-style under some bridge after
dark. Then I'll overhear her telling someone else the same story
but she'd say it was on *top* of the bridge before sunset. Lying
through her muddy braces. A mad house. But I actually started
to enjoy myself…

Rugrat

NOW.

There was this special school trip. For RE. We had to go on a
pilgrimage. A pilgrimage is when you take a walk towards God.
It's meant to bring you closer to the G-man himself. You're
meant to go as you are, imperfect. Some people go with their
sickness, some wanna give thanks and others are just curious.
Us? We were forced to go. Didn't wanna be there to save my
dog's life.

Had to walk some long ting. Proper long. Must've been like
thirty of us trekking through fields and shit. It had rained as
well. And we could proper see the rainbow. We looked up at it –
(*He looks.*) clean across the sky. I swear by the time we looked
back in front of us everyone was gone.

It was just me, Jerome and Baker. Lost.

At first we were scared but then we thought, *'Fuck it.'* The sun
came out and dried everything up quick time. We walked past
some green gardens, cows, some old church. You wouldn't

think there'd be stray cats out in the countryside, would you?
There was. Couldn't believe it. Baker spotted it. He was like –

'Oi, blood, that rabbit looks bizarre.'

(*Sotto*.) He's so dumb.

*'If it's a cat, then what's it doing in the bush? Who takes care of
it?'*

Baker.

Anyway, we kept walking, past farmers and sheep, sheepdogs.
Was kinda therapeutic. It was the first time in our lives that we
just 'walked'.

Ten minutes went by where nobody said nothing, just marching
like.

The sun started rising down. We got to a village. It was dead-
out. Ghost town. We saw some old man walking his little
rat-dog. Weirdest thing though as well, cos I *know* I saw this
one black brudda in the distance. (*Intrigued as he watches him*.)
I got good eyesight, innit, and he defo ain't with us on this
pilgrimage ting. I went to a joke like – (*Turns to get the
attention of his boys*.)

'Yo, Jerome, why's your uncle…'

(*Turning back to the black man*, RUGRAT *is perplexed to find
he's no longer there*.)

Just like that. The brudda wasn't there.

Anyway, we arrived at this old bridge. Stopped in front of it. I
saw it and was like –

'Fuck me, that's an old bridge.'

Kehinde

By Year 10, me and Rachel were still friends but she weren't my girl. The incident with the CRB brought me and Taiwo closer so I didn't need a girlfriend any more after that. But we were still cool though, Rachel and I. We were both taking a few early GCSE's so we went to the library together – things like that. On one evening after the library we went back to hers. We randomly kissed in the library that day and we were gonna do some more at her house or something. Her dad was home, I heard him creak the floorboard upstairs. He didn't mind me being there ever. He came down the stairs slowly when he heard us that day. Caught us as we were mixing Ribena in the kitchen, he told Rachel to leave, she took my Ribena glass with her to the sitting room so I'd join her afterwards, he sat me down at the dinner table and told me that Taiwo had drowned at the lido and that she was in a better place now. He twisted his keys in his hand as he spoke to me. He would drive me home.

When the car stopped at the traffic lights, I jumped out and ran. Ran until I didn't recognise the streets. Until the parked cars looked more expensive. Until the houses got further apart from each other. Until the people were shades paler in colour. Until nothing could remind me of Taiwo.

I just thought I'd feel it, ya know, her being my twin. We Yoruba believe both twins share one soul. So if one twin dies, the soul is disturbed – leaving the other twin unbalanced.

There's this ritual. The making of the Ere Ebeji. It's meant to balance my soul.

The Ifá Priest chooses the best carver from my village back home, one who knew my ancestors. The carver is asked to make an Ere Ebeji; a small wooden figure of Taiwo.

The head was big in proportion to the body because that's where her spirit is transported to. And although it looks nothing like Taiwo, the figure is to be as respected and as powerful as the person it represents.

Grandma treated it as if it were real. She bathed it, fed it, and in the winter, clothed it. On my birthday, it'd be put out on display. Cos it would be her birthday too. And Grandma put it in my school bag on random days. I'd get to first lesson, unzip my bag and find that wooden piece of shit in there and I'd just wanna smash it.

Forgive me, ancestors, Ifá Priest and all believers of the ritual, for I am bold to say the least that it did not balance my soul.

One day, when the world was enough, when I couldn't bear it, when I couldn't get the image of Pierre's clenched teeth as he held my sister's head under the water out of my mind, I went up north to do something stupid. Something very foolish – to myself. Something that only people who hate their lives do. But there, I met a girl. She saved me. She saved me from myself.

You never know who God is gonna take back next, but at the same time you never know who God is gonna bring into your life. Joanne.

Joanne

I slipped in the shower again. This time I had to have my arm in a sling for a week. So while the others went abseiling and did all them DUMB activities, I stayed back at the retreat. Reading. Writing poems a bit. I had that Slum Village tune on religious repeat.

(*Singing.*) '*Being wid you all alone is like a dream come true*' – I can't sing, innit.

I was mentally illing myself in the mirror one day. Just dissecting my – I fucking hate my chin, I was imagining it smaller when Kehinde bussed in. He apologised like a madman for not knocking first. Said he didn't know anyone was here, that I was in his old room –

KEHINDE. So sorry, I used to come here, I'm just helping out this week.

JOANNE. He was from London as well. Whenever he spoke he placed his hand on the back of his neck.

KEHINDE. Have you met Mrs Butler? Did she tell you the story about the boy who never leaves? That's me, innit. I still can't believe she gave you my room, I thought I was exclusive.

JOANNE. I swear he KILLED me with the neck thing. You know when someone does something sweet and then you love them straight away. Everything they do after that is voodoo, just hooks you. I died about ten times speaking with him. I felt like I stumbled across the most humble prince. He's really a duke or a prince but he doesn't know it yet.

(*To* KEHINDE.) Oi, Kehinde, I'm gonna tell you everything about my life and you can tell me what you think, okay?

Rugrat

Was one of them arch bridges made of old grey rocks and that.

We jammed at the middle of the bridge, at its highest point which wasn't that high. It was a small bridge and below on either side, where there probably once was a running stream, was now a house with a garden. Both these houses were derelict. One of the roofs had caved in. Baker starts hanging his upper body over the bridge, peering into one of the houses. Me and Jerome are on the opposite side, just taking in the purple-and-blueberry sky. It's okay. I mean… everything's okay when skies are that colour, innit. Now I'm thinking about that brudda again. Dunno why but I'm thinking deep about him still – I know I didn't imagine it. The way he just disappeared.

I mean he *was* standing kinda close to the cliff edge – well, I looked away and like. Dunno. Maybe he –

'Oi oi oi, you lot, there's a baby over here,' said Baker.

Thing is right. If it was anyone else, you might – MIGHT! – believe them right? They wouldn't randomly say there was a baby out in the woods, and I'm normally not a doubting Thomas, but because it was Baker…

'I swear down, it's… it's a little baby.'

In my heart, deep down, I knew, there wasn't a baby there, there was no such thing. That's one of the stupidest things Baker's ever come with. So Jerome and I blanked him. That was until, we heard what sounded like a noise from a baby.

'Hello, little baby,' said Baker

Jerome and I crossed over to Baker's side of the bridge and to our surprise when you lean your body over the bridge and you look to your left – and if Jerome got his melon head out of the way! – you could see a baby. A baby. In the sticks. Under a bridge. Somewhere up north. We got lost and found a baby. I couldn't imagine that wild shit. I turn to Baker –

'I can see the little baby now.'

'Told you.'

Joanne

Kehinde didn't have much advice. But he listened well and he was honest.

He said I was crazy. To which I replied, *'True indeed, tell me somethin' that I don't already know, blood.'*

Then he said I should write a novel because I got nuff mad stories and dat. My reply to that was – *'Real Talk.'*

Don't know how practical that would be, a fifteen-year-old manic-depressive, fucking... orphan child, writing a booklet for other people to actually read and dat but – *Real Talk*. Cos he had a point, I do have mad testimonies.

He said that I needed to tell Baker I was having his baby. I replied – *'Fuck Off!'* In a venomous rage. Dunno why. Touchy subject, parenthood. Well... with me anyway. It's touchy.

I seriously felt kinda guilty that all because of me... Kehinde had to sleep in a stuffy little cupboard across the hall. It could barely fit a single bed.

Rugrat

Countryside. Up north. Us lot. Lost. On a pilgrimage that we didn't wanna be on. Under a troll's bridge. We see a baby. I was looking at it.

I'm feeling kinda woozy so I quit hanging off this bridge and get back on my feet. Jerome and Baker are still hanging down the side of this bridge. The head rush clears and I scope my surroundings. Not a *soul* in sight. I'm standing on a bridge and there's a baby underneath. Probably directly underneath me. Jesus Christ –

'Oh! That was close,' said Jerome.

'I got it, bruv, what you talking about?' says Baker.

'No you didn't,' said Jerome.

'I did,' says Baker.

Them lot started seeing who can spit on the baby.

(*Spits.*)

'Oh! It's looking at me.'

'Come here, baby.'

(*Spits*.)

Ah man. I dunno. I dunno, a week ago I'd be down there spitting with them.

'*If I was where you are I'd get a bull's eye.*'

'*Come here, little baby.*'

Temperature drop. In both heart and atmosphere. It's getting cold.

'*Look, Baker, the baby's got your fish eyes,*' said Jerome.

'*Shut up… nah wait, Baby does kinda look like me still,*' said Baker.

That's when I automatically blurted out –

'*Him and Jodie had a son!*'

I didn't have to say that. And it burns me that I'm joining in but it naturally just –

'*Him him him and Jodie had a bush baby, innit, you been carrying him all this way, Baker?*'

(*Quickly covers his mouth with his hand before he can say more.*)

They laughed.

'*See look, if that's not my spit on its nose then what?*' says Baker.

'*Rugrat! Where you at?*'

I'm here, man.

I can't watch them. It's not good. They're playing with God. They're spitting on a little helpless baby.

'*Please, oi, you lot, come let's go, man.*'

They stand up straight.

'*Whoa, head rush. Baker, you can't get a head rush, can you?*' said Jerome.

'*Come we just go, man.*'

Baker has this pebble in his hand. He throws it high and catches it –

'I bet you any money that I can dash this on the baby with my eyes closed.'

Joanne

That night, I couldn't sleep. Frankie next door was killing me with the noises, having finger-sex with herself. So I goes up the hall to Kehinde's cupboard-room, quieter there, innit. I stood outside it for about ten minutes. I was stuck. My feet were cemented. I wanted to go in but it had a black door.

Blue door, blue door, blue door, black door.

Kehinde must've felt my presence because he opened up slowly and peeked his head out. Either that or he could see my shadow underneath his door. He assured me I had nothing to worry about and he said that the door was blue underneath, that when he used to come here, the door was blue. He even found a bit on the bottom of the door where the painter had missed a spot. It was baby blue –

KEHINDE. Told you.

JOANNE. He said.

To which I replied –

'Get over it, fam, not like it's the only blue door on planet Earth, fam, it's nothing to congratulate or celebrate, fam, it's not like you've just hit the jackpot, fam – real talk.'

But secretly I was mad relieved that the door was baby blue.

We laid in his small cot. And obviously I've jammed with boys before but Kehinde was on some different echelon. We were communicating on some next wavelength – dolphin frequency. He just starred at me for ages like – right in my eyes like he could see directly to my soul. Like he tapped a channel to my spirit. That's him though, he just looks at me and I'm liquidised – not even on no sexual ting – come like Cyclops Polyphemus the way he be watching me. Well, it felt like that anyway. That's when I clocked he was a blue magnet. Him blue and me red. The way we attracted was as if he already had a magnet vacancy. As if I was filling up a space that was once inhabited. See, just when I thought I had conquered the world of ferromagnetism, behold, Kehinde the blue magnet; cool on the outside and hot in the middle.

He combed his fingers through my hair. And he discovered the scar on my head – (*Indicates a scar, it's in the same region as Taiwo's scar.*)

And I remembered Mum. And he remembered someone. And a tear rolled down my cheek and onto his chest. And I used my finger as the pen, and my tears as the ink, to draw perfect circles on his chest as the canvas. And then a single kiss came down and landed on my head and it was suspended there for a while. He held me tight. And he said –

'Finally.'

(*Touched.*) *'Finally.'* He said *'Finally.'* About *me*. No one's ever waited for me before.

I never knew so many emotions could hit you at the same time. And the thought that there was no guarantee, no promise, that I would ever meet another soul who would hold me like he did that night, made my heart beat out of control like his own. Made my head explode. In that moment, I swear, I was forced to grow the fuck up. I said to myself –

(*In tears.*) *'Jodie. Nah nah. Joanne. You're not a little girl no more, y'understand. You gotta use this – (Points to head.) now. More crucial than ever. No, it hasn't been all roses but move – the fuck – on. You're a big girl. Fuck…'*

I was crying, boy. I don't cry. I never cry. But I was crying – real talk.

Then the following morning, Kehinde, 'the boy who never leaves', had to leave. Abruptly.

Boy.

I don't know what I got that's making them leave. If ever loved by a magnet like Kehinde you have been loved totally. This magnet will pry apart your ribs, ram its hand into your chest cavity, steal all of your heart, and leave the phattest scar 'cross your chest just so's you never forget.

I *could* tell you that him just suddenly leaving didn't take the piss out of my life completely, that it didn't leave me unbalanced, that it didn't relaunch misery.

Rugrat

There's no real reason why Baker wants to stone the baby. No reason.

I look to the end of the bridge and I swear I can see that black brudda.

Just there. He's standing there.

Clocking me. Come like he knew I was thinking of him. But he was behind us though. I ain't got nothing for him.

'Go on then, four pound,' said Jerome.

'Deal,' says Baker.

He's just standing there like.

His shirt is blowing hard in the wind like it was when he was standing near the cliff. But it ain't windy though – what the fuck, man.

Baker throws the stone at the baby.

'OH! That was close, bruv, but you missed, gimme my four pound,' says Jerome.

'Double or nothing.'

'Well, you might as well bring my eight pound right now, fam, deal.'

They shake hands. The atmosphere is ripped. Cold. (*Shivers.*)

But look at this brudda. Can't tell if he's staring me out cos I can't get focus on his eyes, too tough. He's right there but I don't feel if he's there for definite or not. Why am I shook? Why can't I move my feet? Why ain't these lot takin' note of this guy? He's coming closer. I can't…

(*Frightened.*) *'We… we should come off this bridge.'*

Did that even come out? It ricocheted in my head but I bet it didn't come. I feel warm piss run down the inside of my leg.

Baker finds a new stone.

'Ahh what? That's too big!' says Jerome.

'How's it too big?'

'That's a fucking boulder.'

'But go on, I bet you still miss.'

'I'm gonna get it in its face.'

(*Closes his eyes.*)

I wish this guy would disappear. I wish this guy would disappear.

(*Opens his eyes, looks.*)

Wait. I recognise his face.

'Come here, little baby.'

'Nar nar nar, that's cheating, bruv, you can't make the baby come to you, drop it now or the bet's off.'

'Blesssss blesssss blesssss.'

(*Baker drops the rock.*)

(*Long beat.*)

Taruvangadum. It was Mr Taruvangadum. He rushed over with a quickness.

'Sir sir, we found a baby,' said Baker.

'We found a baby, sir,' said Jerome.

'Yo, Rugrat... Rugrat, are you crying, bruv?'

We get to some church where everybody's been waiting for us. The CRB Youngers were there, Terence and dat. We're greeted with a loud cheer that echoes bad. I could hear Babatunde's overloud clap, distorting. Feel like a prodigal son, except I don't want the praise. I got the phattest weight on my chest pinning me down.

Baker's a hero. For finding the baby. He's smiling big. Fucking yellow teeth. The teachers rub his head. He's a fucking nobleman, a crown prince.

'Ah was the one that saw it, innit, they didn't even believe me,' he said.

This guy. Felt like telling him to shut his mouth. Instead I walked up to him and punched him in the face. Twice. They all thought I was crazy. Felt so good though, man. The second punch didn't even connect properly, I think I caught his neck or something but it felt good.

Something weird come over me that day. Had an out-of-body experience. I woke up. I could see where I was in life, and I could distinguish between where I was heading and where I wanted to be. I grew up. We don't grow up on our birthdays, it's on random experiences like this one.

Joanne

Thing is. Nobody saw him but me. No one saw him but me so when I'm telling them he left. I look mad, innit. I sound mental. I'm flippin' out though. Fighting his corner, he's my boy, innit. I'm blowing up. About I'm chatting shit –

'He was here so shut – YES HE *WAS* HERE, close your breath or you're gonna feel a – '

(JOANNE *suddenly lashes out at someone*.)

I have to break Frankie's arm cos she don't believe me. People don't understand though. They all thought I was crazy. I'm jumping round like Ali now. Whoever wants some –

'Cooome. Come, bredrin!'

(*She skips and jumps around in a boxer's stance.*

The CHORUS *slowly close in on her. She puts up a fight but they manage to hold her arms down*.)

This was when I fell to pieces. And this was when more doctors than I knew even existed began trying to piece me back together again.

I ain't crazy.

I'm just hurt.

But try telling them that when you've got half an umbilical cord hanging out of you with no baby to show. Real talk.

He's out there in the world somewhere. It's the magnets. I can feel him still.

He may have disappeared but you know what? The boy never leaves.

(*She touches the back of her neck like* KEHINDE *did, she smiles as they spin her away*.)

EPILOGUE

RUGRAT. As the world gets better at spinning!

JOANNE. We get dizzy and fall on our rare.

KEHINDE. Some keep falling through the atmosphere.

RUGRAT. Some don't survive past 12:05.

KEHINDE. But if you've got *this* – (*Heart*.)

JOANNE. And if you use *this* – (*Brains*.)

RUGRAT. And if you're not afraid of being you.

KEHINDE. If most of what you say is what you do.

JOANNE. Then everyfing is gonna be cool.

RUGRAT. Don't forget your dreams –

KEHINDE. – Dreams that are forgotten do not blossom.

JOANNE. Live, but don't run too fast.

RUGRAT. Play, but don't forget to read.

KEHINDE. Focus, but don't forget to eat.

JOANNE. Love, but keep your nobility – real talk.

RUGRAT. Study, but don't forget to learn.

KEHINDE. Be knowledgeable, but don't forget to listen.

JOANNE. Seek, but don't forget your vision.

RUGRAT. Travel, but be at home with yourself.

ALL. BE YOUNG!

JOANNE. – Be young, you can't forget to be young, so be young, but don't forget to grow –

RUGRAT. – Oh no –

JOANNE. – You gotta grow.

KEHINDE. And strive, but only with self-respect.

JOANNE. When happy see the virtue in sadness.

RUGRAT. When crowded appreciate the peacefulness of loneliness.

KEHINDE. When rich find the hunger poverty-generated.

JOANNE. Aspire, but don't forget to be.

RUGRAT. Aspire, but don't forget to be.

KEHINDE. Aspire, but don't forget to be.

(*Lights to black.*)

ESTATE WALLS

Characters

OBI, *twenty years young*
CAIN, *twenty years old*
MYLES, *nineteen years old*
CHELSEA, *nineteen years old*
REGGIE, *thirty-nine years old*

Setting

Pembury Estate, Hackney, 2009.

Notes

Names appearing without dialogue indicate active silences between characters listed.

/ denotes where dialogue is interrupted.

[ ] denotes where dialogue is spoken at the same time and in non-specific order.

PROLOGUE

Enter OBI, MYLES *and* CAIN.

OBI. I'm on da estate wall!

CAIN. Me too.

MYLES. Me too.

CAIN. On da estate wall.

OBI. And that's where?

MYLES. Right here.

CAIN. Within da estate walls.

OBI. He's back.

CAIN. I'm back!

MYLES. When da world's outside.

OBI. Outside.

CAIN. All I know are these estate walls.

ALL. Estate walls.

MYLES. These cracked windows.

ALL. Estate walls.

OBI. These cracks in my ceiling.

ALL. Estate walls.

CAIN. These cracks that I peep through.

ALL. Estate walls.

MYLES. These cracks on da floor.

ALL. Estate walls.

OBI. You can't jump these cracks.

ALL. Estate walls.

CAIN. You'll get eaten by da crack.

ALL. Estate walls.

MYLES. Feel you bones go CRACK!

ALL. Estate walls.

CAIN. But I love it here.

OBI. Right here?

CAIN. Right here on da estate wall.

MYLES. Me too.

OBI. Me too.

CAIN. On da estate wall.

MYLES. You bored?

OBI. Not at all.

CAIN. How long?

MYLES. All day.

OBI. How far?

CAIN. Bare far.

MYLES. You bored?

OBI. Gettin' bored.

CAIN. How long?

MYLES. Too long.

OBI. How far?

CAIN. This far.

MYLES. Where you at?

OBI. Right here.

CAIN. Right where?

MYLES. At da wall.

OBI. Alone?

CAIN. Never that.

MYLES. Who you with?

CAIN. I'm wid you.

OBI. And me.

MYLES. Obviously.

CAIN. There's three.

OBI. A family.

MYLES. You scared?

CAIN. Don't ask them questions there.

OBI. You scared?

MYLES. Don't ask them questions there.

CAIN. You scared?

OBI. Don't ask them questions there, there's no fear on da estate wall.

CAIN. Not at all.

Scene One

A cool summer day. An estate wall. CAIN, MYLES, *and* OBI.
OBI *has a book.* MYLES' *mobile phone beeps. It's a text message*

MYLES. Message.

This girl's always texting me some emotional lovey-dovey waste messages. Tell me if this makes any sense to you lot.

(*Reading.*) 'Dear Myles, I watched a leaf get blown off its branch today and it reminded me of the time you and I broke up, I'm so glad we're back together xXx :)'

OBI. The girl likes you so she's making an effort.

MYLES. I don't wanna know about no leaf gettin' blown off a twig, b. Why can't she just say 'Hi Myles, I like the way you broke me off last week, can I have round two?' She's always chatting some garbage and because nobody understands it but her, she finks it's deep.

OBI. She's trying to stimulate your mind.

MYLES. Stimulate ma – you know what, you chat to her then. I don't speak in riddles.

OBI. You sure you wanna do that?

CAIN. Handing her over to the merchant of lyrics. That's a sucker move.

OBI. Tell him.

CAIN. Now, there's a certain type of man they say you shouldn't leave your girl around.

OBI. I can out-slick a can of oil.

I can sell water to a well.

Don't leave me round your girl.

MYLES. You could never steal my girl...

OBI. There's no challenge for the ruler.

MYLES. Not even in your wildest, b...

OBI. You're lucky I'm done with that.

MYLES.... 'Cause I'm too pretty.

> I mean look at me! (*Stands, gives us a twirl, his trousers hang low.*) See, Obi, I've been blessed and burdened at the same time. My blessing lies at face value, it's evident – I'm good looking. But my burden... man, so many... I've had so many of those caramel tings that I can't even remember their names... and I ain't proud of that but – that's the way the cookie crumbles.

> My gift is my curse.

> Being beautiful.

> This face is a good look. It's just the way I was born, gotta live with it. But you, Obi, you're one of the lucky ones, I envy you – you'll *never* feel this pain.

OBI. Never?

MYLES. Never. You're too ugly.

CAIN. Oh! Deeep.

OBI. You got jokes.

MYLES. I'm just sayin', you don't wanna go through this, b. I'm the Eighth Wonder of the World, that's a lot to digest every day. Even the way my hair grows is unique, it grows that way, like feng shui – to the east or something... or north... I don't care, the girls love it.

> OBI *disregards* MYLES *and gets back to reading his book.*

> Your sister knows – she is drunk off of love potion for me.

> OBI *gestures in disapproval.*

> Don't think your sister's an angel, ya know. You don't know what your sister gets up to when you're not about. (*Grabbing his crotch and nudging* CAIN.) *I* do.

CAIN (*stirring and laughing*). Oh no! Don't have it.

OBI. Come off my sister please.

MYLES. No but, b, you need to come to grips with something though, 'cause you always talk about your sister like she's a saint. Bruv, that girl is seventeen – SEVENTEEN. Dat's the age that make girls do mad shit and experiment – remember? Her hormones are running high right now – *sex* hormones. Them the ones that make you wanna have sex and shit.

OBI. Do you wanna shut your mouth?

CAIN. Don't let him roast your sister.

MYLES. Bruv, brother, b, don't act like you don't see your sister walking up and down the estate looking freshhhh.

Fresh to death.

Fresh to her bone marrow.

That girl always looks magnetic.

Sometimes I think this estate was built over an ancient burial ground and she's one of the ghosts 'cause when she walks she floats.

But where's she going?

OBI. She's going college innit – leave it.

MYLES. That's what she wants you to think, b! Do you see her going into the college gates? No. All you see is her leaving the estate and unless you're following her you can't tell me she's not skipping classes to link up with one of those sweet boys, one of those sweet-like-chocolate boys, getting greasy with one of them boys. Even the good girls do it every once in a while. Face the facts, rude boi, your sister's no different from the rest of us.

OBI (*snapping*). Look, you haven't got a sister. But maybe one day – one day if you're lucky enough you'll have a daughter, then you can see if it's easy to face the facts...

MYLES. [Ahh here we go...]

OBI. ...nar nar listen though 'cause you wanna discuss. I know how tings are, I was seventeen too. But for my peace of mind, my little sister, I'd rather believe that she's been going college every day. Is that alright? Is that okay with you, Mr Jeremy Kyle?

MYLES. Hmm. But she needs to stop looking at me like the way she do though, I'm too old for her.

OBI *ignores* MYLES *and reads his book.*

MYLES *snatches the book from* OBI *and holds it away from him.*

OBI. Oi what the fff... blood, stop stop stop seriously I mean it.

MYLES. Easy nah.

OBI. Send my book!

MYLES. Calm down. What you got in this ting anyway?

OBI. Just give it.

MYLES *opens the book to read a page. They scrap over the book.*

You know I could easily knock you out innit?!

MYLES. Cain, you see this book, all since last year Obi's been /

OBI. / Shut up! /

MYLES. / OBI'S BEEN writing stuff, secrets and shit.

CAIN. Izit now?

MYLES. He don't let no one see.

CAIN. What's in the book?

OBI. Pass it.

MYLES. Nope.

They wrestle over the book.

[Er don't grab my bum, you batty-man, ahh you touched my balls bruv, er, move man, you're bent.]

OBI. [Pass it. Pass da book. Do you want me to knock you out?]

MYLES *breaks free and stands behind* CAIN.

Cain.

CAIN. You should know not to keep secrets. I'm a nosy guy.

MYLES. And me.

CAIN. Read it.

MYLES. Easy.

MYLES *clears his throat*.

OBI. Don't.

MYLES (*reads*). I'm... I'm twenty... twenty years young.
But I feel older.
So, I'm twenty years young but I feel older.
I'm twenty years young but I feel older.
Is it because children of the in... inferior grow up quicker?
So, is it because children of the inferior grow up quicker?
Experiences maybe.
But I still... still believe.
I'm an ex... ex... exception to the rule.
So, but I still believe I'm an exception to the rule.
Because looking out my... looking out OF my window.
All I see is... all I see is... all I see is – (*Squinting his eyes to read.*) /

OBI. /... crime in da ghetto.

OBI *snatches his book back*.

All I see is crime in da ghetto. You're killing it, man.

MYLES. Book.

OBI. 'Cause you don't read enough.

MYLES. I'll have you know I read about FIFTEEN text messages per day. Pass da book.

OBI. You read like your brain's about to combust.

CAIN. Demonstrate, Obi. Show him how it's 'posed to sound.

OBI. You ain't ready.

MYLES. See! 'Cause you know I'm a better reader than you.

OBI *makes to leave.*

CAIN. Read it, man.

OBI. 'Tis too-too deep for thine ears.

CAIN. I'm a deep guy.

OBI. Myles, you almost ripped out one of my pages, you waste-man!

MYLES. Did I? Sorry, b. Forgive me, sire, more-times I'm ever so clumsy.

OBI. Yeah. Your mum.

MYLES. Thank you, sir.

OBI *leaves.*

MYLES *smiles craftily, watches him leave then turns around to* CAIN:

Look what I got, b. He didn't even know I took it.

He presents from his pocket a rumpled page from OBI'*s book.*

Oi, read it for me. I kinda like what he was sayin' in that other one.

About, 'I'm twenty years young'... see most people would say they're twenty years old innit? Do you get it?

CAIN. Do *you* get it?

MYLES. C'mon, b, just read it for me. Look it ain't even that long... less than half a page, b.

CAIN. Lemme see da ting.

MYLES *straightens the page and hands it over to* CAIN. CAIN *looks at the page, looks at* MYLES, *then turns the page the right way up.*

MYLES. Read it out loud innit.

CAIN *reads the first couple of lines in his head. He chuckles to himself.*

I… I can't hear you reading it.

CAIN (*annoyed*). Sekkle down, man.

MYLES. Nah cos like, share the experience innit that's all I'm saying, b /

CAIN. / Know what, go stand way over there, man, I can't have you leaning over my shoulder like some English teacher y'understand.

MYLES *indignantly walks to the other side of the wall.*

MYLES. Read it from the top.

With the title and all-dat.

I wanna get the full effect.

CAIN. The title is 'She Understands Me'.

(*Reading.*) She understands me
She puts the wind in my sails
But most of all she understands me
She shadows me not
Because she understands me
So shades me instead
By understanding me in a world of perplexity

Her body is so smooth
That I cannot remember whether she has a belly button
But most of all she understands me
My hands agree with her cup size
My lips agree with her neck
My nose agrees with every scent she has to offer
And every scent they find via intrusion
And my cameras
My cameras
I never turn my cameras off
Even when she sleep beside me I'm zooming in
And as if all that isn't enough
On top of all that cake
She and I fit like jigsaw

But the sun can't light the whole world at one time
Her fruit are forbidden
I must keep my urges well hidden

OBI *enters. He hears the last few lines.*

Maybe I don't feel brave enough to tell you any of this
Maybe I'll stop loving you, on December the 32nd
Maybe you are my life support
Maybe without you my whole being goes beep beep
beeeeeeeeeeee...

OBI *recognises his work and panics, snatching the paper out of* CAIN*'s hand:*

OBI. Where'd you get this?

MYLES (*thrilled*). I took it out your book without you knowing but, b – you got some new-found respect, b, I'm a fan, b.

OBI. You can't go stealing my stuff!

MYLES. But, b! That was out of this world, b!

CAIN. It wasn't bad. A few words were spelt wrong.

OBI. I know, that's the style.

MYLES (*excited*). That's his style, b – leave him be, b. It's not lyrics though is it?

OBI. Well...

CAIN. It's a poem.

MYLES. A poem? Yo regardless of how gay that sounds, just run with dat, rude boi, you put your heart on that page like a... like a...

OBI. Yeah I got you, cool your breeze... just don't go stealing my stuff. It's private.

CAIN. Who was it about though?

MYLES. Yeah. Who is she?

OBI. She's...

MYLES. You could tell us, man.

CAIN. Yeah. Why couldn't you have her?

OBI. She's…

MYLES. Why was she forbidden?

OBI. She's no one… nobody… She's not even real…

MYLES. Did you bang her?

OBI. No, Myles.

   I didn't bang her.

MYLES. You should bang her, b.

OBI. She only exists in a world suspended in time. I made it up.

MYLES. *Beep beep beeeeeeeeeeeep*. Shit was *deeeeep*! It
   sounded like a life-support machine in da hospital innit. B,
   that girl is real and you love her.

CAIN. My first day back on the estate and Obi's in *love*.

OBI. What? Nar.

MYLES. You love her!

CAIN. He just don't wanna say who she is.

MYLES. Da poetry though, Obi, you've found something
   original. See, I gotta find *my* shit.

CAIN. Don't let her read dat poem, she'll run a mile with it.

MYLES (*to himself*). I *could* do poetry as well. Nar, that's batty.
   Maybe…

CAIN. She'll make you look stupid.

MYLES.…maybe journalism.

CAIN. By all means, show 'em a little affection but don't write
   'em poetry. That's for pussies.

MYLES. Nar that won't work, too much writing.

CAIN. Real men don't spill their hearts out like that for no
   woman.

OBI. It's a poem.

CAIN. But exactly. Since when did you write poetry, rude boi?

MYLES. Oi look, there's your lil sister, Obi.

They look out into the estate complex.

Tell her to come say hello.

OBI *kisses his teeth.*

MYLES (*to* OBI*'s sister*). Ay!… You cool?! Right, right. I'll see you about innit! (You-are-peng; one day.) How the sun doth shine off of dat gyal like she is forever walking into the sunse – see what your poetry is doing to me, blood?! I'm already affected like.

He watches her leave, he spots something.

Black Punto! Black Punto! You know whose car that is innit, look!

CAIN. I see him still.

MYLES. Oi!

CAIN. Trying to show everyone that he can come out of prison and have a car waiting for him. That's okay, he can drive in circles but he ain't going nowhere.

OBI. Did he just get out today as well?

CAIN. Nah he got a couple months shaved off of his sentence. Fuckin' snitch.

MYLES. So what, you gonna heat him up?

CAIN. Not even. What good is he to me if I mash him up straight away? Delvin owes me now, he's in my debt. I'm gonna get him to sell white for my uncle for one year, after that –

(*Chillingly.*) I'll send him an angel in the morning.

MYLES. That's cold.

OBI (*dubiously*). Your uncle's cool with this?

CAIN. Man, he phoned me when I was locked up and said 'nephew that's a sick idea'.

MYLES. That is cold!

CAIN. Obviously I trust you two mans to keep this our little secret.

MYLES. Fucking cold, blood!

MYLES *excited crashes fists with* CAIN.

CAIN. Calm down.

OBI. What makes you think he's gonna sell for your uncle?

CAIN. He wouldn't dare to piss about with Uncle Che.

OBI. You say that like you don't already know the boy's a snitch. Cain, you just got out this morning…

CAIN. I know, I'm a year behind I need to catch up right?

OBI. What you *need* to do is slow down.

Who da fuck is this?

MYLES. Ptshh…

CAIN. Anyway, I'm about ready to feel some paper in my hand.

OBI. Yeah but that's your uncle's money though, it's not like he's selling for you.

CAIN. Uncle Che says when I do this ting I get a hundred per cent of the proceeds – a little starter gift to welcome me to da *big* business.

MYLES. What?!

CAIN. I got nothing to lose, man.

MYLES. Hold tight, Uncle Che, ya know, he's bare safe – all of it?

CAIN. Bruv, all I gotta do is pick up my money every week, all he's gotta do is make sure he has my money. Every week – Friday – cash – that's it! It's not complicated. White ain't hard to sell, these businessmen need their fix and when the year's up and Delvin the green snitch has payed his dues. (*Assembles two fingers to resemble a gun and extends his arm forward.*)

BOOP!

BOOP!

BOOP!

…It's nothing long, I'm a bad man you get me? It's a quick ting – easy. My uncle even offered to get one of his goons to do it for me but nah, bruv, if I wanna be a general I gotta earn some stripes – man should do it himself, I lie? And watch in South London they'll say '*I heard it was that East London breda from Pembrey Estate, Cain, he's a cold-blooded one, don't cross him sideways, you'll have a problem… Complications.*' Goin' on raucous, blood. I ain't no water-pistol-yielding paper soldier. I'm a true marksman, blood. When I talk about it, I be about it. Me and my uncle – big fish y'understand – heavyweights. He moves more pounds of coke than sand at the seaside. From now on, whoever tries bringin' anything to me is gonna be sleeping in the gutter, standard procedures. I've been nice up until now, I've been dat cool breda, but mans start taking that for a weakness – start acting brave and all dat, I lie? Thinkin' they could speak to you anyhow. I won't have a bar of it. Gotta be ruthless out here. Get as much as you can get, shovel as much as you can shovel – by any means necessary. And never let your guard down 'cause as quick as you part your lips open to smile, you'll have a man reaching down your throat to steal the food out of your stomach – you won't even know what hit you it'll happen so fast. I swear, in a moment of weakness I actually thought about going out and getting a normal job or something, stupid right? It's mental what dumb things you think about in prison. Too much time to think. When you're stuck in that room them four walls start chatting to you like four bredrins.

OBI. You could go back to prison.

MYLES (*electrified*). Errr! I love a dirty plan!

CAIN (*to* MYLES). I'm grimy like that – put faith in me like you do Jesus, rude boi. I've always got a plan, naturally.

MYLES. 'Cause if you ain't got a plan, you're not a man.

CAIN. You know this.

MYLES. B. You changed, b. I love the way you think now –
I wanna go prison, b – come back and start thinking more
like you. Does Delvin know?

CAIN. Nah not yet.

MYLES. What are you waiting for, man? You got money to be
making.

CAIN. When you're ready innit.

MYLES *is baffled*.

When you're ready – What, don't you wanna make some
dough with me no?

MYLES (*fired up*). Yeah, I'm good for that! Ha ha.

CAIN. But you gotta cool your foot, man – it's a silent
operation.

MYLES (*whispering*). Trust – man can do silent operations, b.

OBI *frowns on the whole idea. He has disconnected himself
from the conversation*.

CAIN. Obi One – he doesn't wanna get his hands dirty.
Remember that lyric he wrote back in the day, '*It's Obi One,
I'm so greeeeasy, pull up sleeeeevy, I ain't greedy but who'd
have thought jacking phones was this eeeeasy…*'

MYLES. '*… the dark lord with the sharp sword, you might've
seen me on C-C-Teeeee-V, 'cause da cameras be watching,
da cameras be watching, da cameras be watching meee…*'

CAIN. Obi One, we're gonna need you to supervise the
manoeuvre – just like old times.

OBI. You don't need me.

CAIN. Obviously we do 'cause when we go see Delvin, we're
gonna need *the dark lord with the sharp sword* – that's you.
Remember, you'd always carry the knife, police never search
you 'cause how you look, and you don't walk like us – you
could get away with murder.

MYLES. If he don't wanna do it I can be the dark lord.

OBI. Myles, you're not doing it.

CAIN. So you're gonna do it then?

OBI. No, but I ain't letting Myles do it either.

MYLES. Don't talk for me, b, you ain't my guardian.

OBI. Bruv, are you *trying* to go to prison?

MYLES. Of course I am, What'd you think I just said, b?

CAIN. Look, Obi, we used to do this back in the day, it was nothing.

OBI. I'm not on those mad tings any more.

CAIN. So what, you're gonna go legit – that's what you're saying?

OBI *shrugs his shoulders*.

MYLES. Hold up, *you're* going legit?

OBI. I'm doing the straight-and-narrow thing.

CAIN. Seriously?

MYLES. And then there were two…

CAIN. You're gonna go legit?

OBI. Yeah.

MYLES. So are you gonna. Like. Get like. A proper. Like – normal job?

OBI. Something like that.

The boys burst out laughing.

MYLES. So you gonna. Like. Wear like. A proper. Like – McDonald's uniform with the hat?

They crash into laughter.

OBI. A submarine engineer.

CAIN. Huh?

OBI. Submarine engineer. For the Royal Navy. That's what I'm gonna be.

MYLES *and* CAIN *burst out laughing*.

I… and you're laughing… see, cool, nah that hurt me innit. [I'm serious, get off me.]

CAIN. [Oh dear! Ahh sorry but.] Fuck me.

MYLES. Fuck me too, b.

CAIN. I swear you have to study for that.

OBI. I start in September.

CAIN. Shit. I go away for a year… you proper changed, man.

MYLES. Told you.

CAIN. Tell me you're joking, bruv – Okay, you got me, it was funny. Submarines, that's funny.

OBI. You know what, I knew you wouldn't understand.

CAIN. Understand what? Tell it. Show us the way innit.

MYLES. Innit.

OBI. I don't have to show you nothing just open your eyes. See what's *gwarnin* around you.

CAIN. What's *gwarnin*?

OBI. What's *gwarnin*? Three weeks ago Jermaine got shot and he died – his mum's losing it, that's both of her sons now. Ronnie's in prison, Shaun got stabbed, Gavin's in prison, Terrance is flippin' – flippin' smoking crack now.

MYLES *and* CAIN *laugh*.

Why you laughing? It's not funny. Any one of them could be you. Everyone's just getting mash-up, no one's moving forward. Jeffrey – where's Jeffrey, bruv? No one even knows where he is – he could be rotting in a sewer for all we know. I don't want my mum to go to my funeral. I don't wanna have roses put down on the roadside for me. I'm not trying to see my Year 7 picture in the *Hackney Gazette*. One life to live. If I don't switch tings up now yeah, it's just a recipe to

mash up the rest of my days. Just – end up getting shot or
something – like the rest of these wannabe gangsters.

CAIN. Do you think *I'm* a wannabe gangster? In fact, don't
answer that – I might switch.

OBI. You might switch? On who?

CAIN. On you.

OBI. Shuut up.

CAIN. Strike one.

OBI. What, 'cause I wanna do my own thing, is that what's
making you rise up out your seat throwing strikes and shit?
You fool.

CAIN. Strike two. Don't get beside yourself, boy.

MYLES. Oi… we're cool.

OBI. My name's Obi y'understand, Obi ONE. One. Dat means
I'm my *own* person. I don't need your affirmation or support
for nothing ya hear. I make moves – I don't consult with or
answer to no one. What *I* eat don't make *you* shit. I'm just
trying to show you something, bruv, I'm trying to show you
'cause clearly you lot still think it's a game. We're always
hearing stories about things happening in other estates, to
people we know, and you two must be knackered if it don't
ever cross your mind that one day that could be you. That
story could be about you, man! I'm doing my own thing. No
one's gonna live my life for me.

Pause.

MYLES *and* CAIN *nod at each other.*

MYLES. Told you.

CAIN. Definitely changed.

MYLES. Told you.

OBI. Yeah I've changed, so? At least I'm trying to get out of
this shithole – get a degree and it's Sunday morning after
that – they see my little degree – get hired quick.

CAIN. 'Cept, you're forgetting how many people have tried
that shit. All them years of hard work squashed into one
paper and that paper won't even help you – ESPECIALLY
when you're black.

MYLES. Yeah, man, that's true.

OBI. See I *knew* you'd do that.

CAIN. Do what?

OBI. You're playing the race card, fam.

CAIN. How's that, fam?

OBI. You're making it a black–white thing, you always do
that…

CAIN. It's not a black–white thing, I ain't got nothing against
them. I pray to a white God. When I close my eyes and
I picture God, he's some old white man, with white hair and
a long white beard…

MYLES. Bruv, that's Santa Claus.

CAIN.…So, it's not a race thing. It's a 'being black' thing.
Black boys like us haven't had a chance from day one –
don't you know that being black is a handicap? It's like
being in a wheelchair you can't do everything – you're
restricted. When you're guilty of being black there ain't all
that many options…

MYLES. Innit though.

CAIN.…We're the last ones hired and the first ones fired.
That's why I do what I do – to get ahead. On da road
I determine how much *I* get paid, depending on how much
grafting and hustling and fixing *I* wanna do – no one hires
me, I'm already high! Ya know, I know I'm black…

MYLES. Preach!

CAIN.…and I know… I know I can't be whatever I wanna
be…

MYLES. Take him to church.

CAIN.…Fuck, I wanna be a chef, but my hands are black – that means that they're dirty. Why, what white man would eat his salad after seeing it being prepared by black hands? But listen, I *could* be a chef, they'd give us that, because it's behind closed doors, literally, nobody sees the chef. But that don't mean, Obi, that don't mean I won't have to work extra-hard to show these people hiring me that I'm hygienic, that these hands are black of pigment and not of grime and filth. You ain't even stepped out into the real world, little brother, reality's a tough pill to take. You wouldn't know about having to fend for yourself, you ain't been there. I was nine years old when I came back from school to find nobody home. When you lot were playing with your Pokémon cards and Tamagotchis, I was forced to grow up as fast as I could. I've *been* grown.

CAIN, MYLES *and* OBI *all look to stage left, simultaneously sidetracked by the sound of a man singing at the top of his infected lungs. It's* REGGIE, *the estate crack addict.*

Enter REGGIE. *He has on his feet a pair of brand-new white Nike Airs.*

REGGIE (*singing*). Three ghetto youts on de estate wall, whole day pass dey do na'ting at all, dey fink dey bad 'cause dey fightin' 'n' brawlin' but one of dese mornin', one of dese mornin', one of dese mornin', one of dese mornin', one of dese mornin', one of dese mornin'

BOOP!

BOOP!

BOOP!

He pretend-shoots each of them with his crusty fingers and succumbs to a hysterical laugh-cough.

MYLES (*wagging his head*). Disgusting.

REGGIE. Why you man look like you seen a ghost? Is my singing that bad?

MYLES. Why are you always disturbing the whole world?

REGGIE. Reggie don't bother nobody. Cain, you're back!

MYLES. Coming round here making up noise – I don't wanna see your tonsils, b.

REGGIE. It's a free country if I wanna *siiiing* /

MYLES. / *SHUT!* your mouth.

The boys laugh. OBI *stifles his laughter.*

OBI. Leave him alone, man.

MYLES. We ain't got no crack for you so be on your way, Reggie.

REGGIE. Cain, have you got a lighter?

CAIN *gives* REGGIE *the lighter to light his cigarette. He nudges* MYLES *and makes a gesture towards* REGGIE*'s new trainers.*

MYLES *brings out his camera-phone and films* REGGIE.

MYLES. Now now – Reggie, you're a crackhead what are you doing with fresh Nike Airs?

REGGIE *discreetly slips* CAIN*'s lighter into his pocket.*

REGGIE. Are you filming?

MYLES. Who'd you kill for those, b – your trainers, b.

REGGIE. Oh these babies? You wanna buy them? I'm just taking them out for a test drive – I'll put them back in the box and they're yours, twenty pound.

MYLES. I ain't buying them.

REGGIE. Fifteen.

MYLES. They don't fit my East-London-player-listic style.

REGGIE. Ten.

MYLES. What size are they?

MYLES *examines the trainers closer, filming them with his camera-phone, using the zoom like a magnifying glass.*

REGGIE. Eight. Fifteen knockers and they're yours right now –
I'll walk home bare feet.

MYLES. You just said ten I got it on camera. Phone.

REGGIE. If you want them right now it's fifteen and I'll walk
home bare feet.

MYLES. You only live upstairs.

REGGIE. Fucking hell give me a break it's just fifteen pound,
no skin off your nose, mate.

MYLES. Ten pound, bruv!!

REGGIE. Well, you can forget it.

MYLES. Cool.

MYLES *calls his bluff.*

REGGIE. Alright alright – I'll be back down in a minute I'll
just put them back in the box.

MYLES *has an epiphany.*

MYLES. Oh my *bludclot* days, it just hit me, I've found my
thing! I found it… I'll make a documentary! All filmed on
the camera-phone. Just like this…

REGGIE *begins to make his way offstage, funny-walking
crackhead style,* CAIN *stops him.*

MYLES *turns his camera-phone on and films the whole
thing.*

CAIN. Reggie. Where are you going?

REGGIE. I just said – I'm up to the flat and I'll be back in a sec.

CAIN. Yeah?

REGGIE *(nervous).* Yeah that's what I just said – didn't I?

CAIN. Where's my lighter?

REGGIE *laughs it off and throws the lighter over to* CAIN.

Try that shit again – I dare you.

REGGIE *rolls his eyes*.

Don't roll your eyes at me. Do you know what happened to the last guy who rolled his eyes at me? They rolled back into his head, then his head rolled back into his neck, then his neck rolled back into his chest and then his chest collapsed. And all that was left was his shoes. I took, those shoes. They were too small. 'Cause I'm a big man. Don't roll your eyes at big men.

MYLES. CUT! Woo… That was hotttt, b. Electrifying. I wanna do it again from another angle so I can cut away from different shots. Cain you was great, I loved it… the whole eyes-rolling thing? We'll keep that in. Focus, Obi, you were giving me nothing…

REGGIE *turns back around to the boys once more*.

REGGIE. Listen, do any of you wanna buy a gun?

The boys burst into laughter.

MYLES. Wait wait… say that again, I wasn't filming.

CAIN. You ain't got no gun to be selling.

MYLES (*filming*). You think we're dumb?

REGGIE. I've got things – if you want something let me know I might be able to get it for the right price.

MYLES. What gun is it?

REGGIE. What do you mean what gun? It's black with a er… round the er…

CAIN. AK-47 automatic assault rifle? 9-milli – what is it?

REGGIE. Well – It got erm… the bullets are bronze at the top and err…

MYLES. MAC-10?

REGGIE. I don't know! It's like – it can fit in your hand.

MYLES *and* CAIN *look at each other. They perform something, an inside joke that they've done for years*.

CAIN *and* MYLES (*singing*). *We don't believe youuuu.*

REGGIE. Well, if you want /

CAIN *and* MYLES (*singing*). *We don't believe youuuu.*

REGGIE. If you want it it's already sorted.

Okay?

Pause.

MYLES. B, why are you still wearing my trainers? I'm gonna start taking one pound off of every five seconds that you're wearing them. Five-four-three…

REGGIE. I'll be down in five!

REGGIE *leaves.*

MYLES. Do you really think he's got a gun?

CAIN. Don't be stupid, he's a crackhead.

OBI. Probably has a toy gun.

MYLES. This documentary is gonna be SICK. I'll call it *Council Estate of Mind* – what the estate'll do to a maaan, when his skin is braaan, in East London taaan.

MYLES' *phone rings. He checks the caller ID.*

(*Dancing.*) *'Oh oh, it's da hotline, 'cause I'm hot boy, emails jam up my Hotmail account 'cause I'm a hot male.'* This girl loooves me, man.

OBI. Who's that?

MYLES. You don't know her.

He answers his phone.

Talk to me, baby.

OBI. What's her name? What's her name? What's her name? Myles.

MYLES. Hold on – (*To phone.*) Brother Obi One, I'm on the phone right now – allow me, b.

OBI. What's her name?

MYLES. You don't know her, she doesn't chat to mans like you.

OBI. Why?

MYLES. 'Cause she's buff that's why she's chatting to me.

OBI. I might know her, what's her name.

MYLES (*reluctantly*). Channy.

Now leave me alone.

(*To phone*.) Hello.

OBI. Chanel?

MYLES. Obviously – that's obviously her full name, b – it's like people call her Channy innit – for short.

(*To phone*.) Yeah hello.

OBI. What ends is she from?

MYLES. Why, why do you do this? You're always wrong.

OBI. She's from Leytonstone innit?

Pause.

MYLES. What, do you know her?

OBI. She's fat, man.

CAIN. Oh!

MYLES *covers the phone*.

MYLES. Nar nar, she's just a bit chubby.

OBI. She's colossal – you said she was buff just now!

MYLES. She *is* buff. [Kinda. Nar why are you exaggerating, Cain, trust me, she ain't even that big, he's exaggerating. She got a pretty face she looks like erm… Jennifer Hudson.]

OBI. [How's she buff? You must mean her body is FAT! Don't lie to yourself.]

CAIN. [Myles got himself a fatty girl. Fatty fatty girl. Ey, don't feel too bad, big girls need love too.]

MYLES (*in denial*). Nah nah nah – come off it, it's cool anyway I just tell her to give me head – get me – that's it.

THAT IS IT!

I wouldn't bang her.

Sex *her*?

Nar, are you mad?

NEVER!

Errr that's nasty, b.

Ha ha.

Nope, not me.

Ha.

CAIN *and* OBI (*singing*). *We don't believe youuuu.*

CAIN. Someone's gotta do it…

OBI.…and if that's what you're in to…

CAIN.…that's what you're in to…

OBII.… Spread love…

CAIN.…all over that fat BIATCHH /

MYLES. / Oi oi seriously, do you wanna hold your mouth?

CAIN. Shut up.

MYLES. Nar, don't tell me to shut up y'understand.

CAIN. Why are you acting all brave 'cause you've got someone on the phone?

MYLES. Both of your mums.

Hello… hello? (*To phone, but there is nobody on the other end.*) See! That's why you lot don't get any pussy – 'cause you don't know how to behave. Animals.

OBI. Not even the fat girls want him.

MYLES. *Not even fat girls want him*, your mum don't want you.

OBI. Aww, don't cry, man, I'm joking.

MYLES *makes to leave*.

Where you going, babe?

MYLES. Not that it's any of your business but I'm gonna go wet my beak.

CAIN. Wet your beak?

MYLES. Yep, something you two probably ain't done in a while with your desert dicks.

OBI. You got a condom? You might spread your diseases.

MYLES. Har-de-har-har funny. She's on the pill, bruv, so hush your gums /

OBI. / The pill don't stop diseases, you moose.

MYLES. Ahh you ain't my dad so don't try and school me. I know what I'm doing.

OBI. Cool.

Tell Chanel I said hi.

MYLES. –

OBI. I thought you said you ain't banging Chanel.

MYLES. Did I just now tell you I'm banging her though?

Did I say that?

No.

OBI. So why's she on the pill?

MYLES. How do you know it's *Chanel* that's on the pill?

Did I just now say *Chanel* is gonna wet my beak? Did I say that? No.

[Think you're smart innit.]

OBI. [Cool cool cool – chill.] Go and erm… splash your beak or whatever.

MYLES (*leaving*). All up in my business like da FBI…

Yo, Cain, it's good to have you back innit.

MYLES *exits*.

CAIN. So. Who is she?

OBI. Who's who?

CAIN. You ain't gotta pretend, you can tell me.

OBI. Tell you what?

CAIN. Who's the chick that's made you all soft, writing love poems and shit.

OBI. Ptshh..

CAIN. Man. Stop it ya know.

OBI. Stop what?

CAIN. Being a pussy, I feel like we're losing you, bro.

OBI. I'm here, man.

CAIN *sees someone out in the estate complex*.

CAIN. Yo! Yo, Chelsea! Chelsea!

OBI. She didn't hear you.

CAIN. I'm seeing her tonight anyway. That's cool.

Feels good to be back. Still feels kinda weird though, feels like I'm standing on one leg.

OBI. Wait, you actually haven't been to see her yet?

CAIN. Ah? Who, Chels? Nah. Wanted to see my boys first innit, da fam-lay!

OBI. Whatever.

CAIN. What?

OBI. Ya scared?

CAIN. Don't ask them questions there.

OBI. 'Cause you could've seen her already, you got back this morning she lives right there /

CAIN. / I know where she lives – who you telling?

I'm just…

OBI. Oh.

I see.

You're nervous.

CAIN. What? Why would I be nervous?

Pause.

Should I be nervous?

OBI. You have been gone a whole year, man.

CAIN. So?

OBI. Many things can change in a year.

CAIN. Well she called me earlier and she sounds the same.

OBI. You heard she's working at the youth club now, putting the youngsters on the right path.

CAIN. Man, the only thing youth club ever taught me was how to play table tennis and even then, I had four dudes waiting ahead of me. I got my wisdom out here, on the blocks. And that's where the youngsters are gonna get it from as well.

REGGIE *enters with a dented Nike shoebox pressed under his arm.*

REGGIE. Where's your boy?

OBI. You just missed him.

REGGIE. Fuck's sake! When's he coming back?

OBI. Not for a long minute. Come and check for him tomorrow.

REGGIE. And give him all that time to change his mind? No thanks.

OBI. Well he ain't here right now.

REGGIE. Christ's sakes. Tell you what I'll do, I'm just gonna leave them here. Okay?

OBI. You could do whatever you want, Reggie.

REGGIE. I'll leave them here – he'll pay me tomorrow. Sweet.

REGGIE *places the shoebox between* CAIN *and* OBI *on the wall and then exits.*

OBI *gets up to leave.*

OBI. Tomorrow.

CAIN. You're lucky 'cause you're like a little brother to me.

OBI. Little brother.

CAIN. Seriously though. If you were anyone else I'd have punched you up for being such a pussy. About your going legit... There's three, and without you the foundation collapses maybe. So quit sucking your thumb. Delvin? That's... that's a minor.

Tomorrow.

CAIN *leaves.*

OBI *grabs the Nike shoebox off of the wall and exits.*

Scene Two

Later that evening. We hear the few children that still play out in the estate complex. We hear a police siren go by. CAIN *and* CHELSEA *sit at the wall.*

CHELSEA. You look good.

CAIN. You… you look same.

CHELSEA. Right.

CAIN. Nah not like, I'm not saying you don't look good… I mean, you always looked good, *look* good, I wouldn't exactly go out with you if you were butterz…

CHELSEA. Keep digging.

CAIN.…Not saying that if you *were* butterz (which you aren't) I wouldn't be with you. I'm just saying that you look the same, like how I remembered you in my mind. And that's good.

CHELSEA. Right.

Pause.

CAIN. D'you wanna come up?

CHELSEA. Why?

CAIN. I gotta go up soon.

He lifts up his trouser leg, revealing an electronic tag on his ankle.

CHELSEA. And whose fault is that?

CAIN. They got me on lockdown. 9 p.m. every day for ninety fuckin' days – (*Attempts to remove the tag.*) But it's okay… 'cause… if I twist it… and I turn my ankle at the same time…

CHELSEA. What you doing?

CAIN. Almost got it off this morning. (*Fiddles around with it.*) Come we go upstairs.

He attempts to usher her, CHELSEA *remains seated.*

CHELSEA. –

CAIN. Why you being all moody? I just got back I ain't even done anything yet.

Let's go upstairs and you can greet your man properly okay.

CHELSEA. The whole day pass today, you jammed here with your boys, the whole afternoon, not once did you come up to see me, not once.

CAIN. See, what had happened was, I had *tried* to summon you, I said 'Yo Chels' but you were power-walking for London...

CHELSEA. Cain, You waited for the sun to go down. You had the whole day. Is that what this is? Am I your night-time flex?

CAIN. You are my night-time, daytime and breakfast-time flex, Chels, but you gotta understand those are my *boy* boys. I gotta check them before I check you. It's an unspoken rule. Them two, that's the only family I got.

Pause.

Well, look my bedroom's tidy – I don't know how long it's gonna last, Chels, let's make the most of it.

CHELSEA. Why don't you ever come to mine?

CAIN. Your... (*Laughs.*) You know I don't go to your flat.

CHELSEA. Something wrong with my flat?

CAIN (*extending his arms like Frankenstein's monster*). It's Fred. Freddy Krueger.

CHELSEA. You're so rude.

CAIN. Fred's crazy.

CHELSEA. I told you don't say that, he's not crazy.

CAIN. So why do I always see him doing some *zoongness*?

CHELSEA (*baffled*). Zoongness? What?

CAIN. He always looks like he's *zoonged* out.

CHELSEA (*smiles*). Zoonged out – Cain?

CAIN (*grins*). Zoonged out of his mind.

CHELSEA. And what exactly might 'zoonged' out mean?

CAIN. Zoonged out innit – It means like… like-he-ain't-enough-getting-to-the-brain-that-oxygen.

CHELSEA (*laughs*). You're just making this up.

CAIN. I'm serious. You tellin' me you've never heard of zoonged out before?

CHELSEA. No.

CAIN. You're late – let me break it down for you, the history of the word *zoong*. Alright, when you roll up weed in Rizla what do you call it?

CHELSEA. Weed – don't you just call it weed? Like, *I'm smoking weed*.

CAIN. No you say *I'm bunning a zoot*. (*Smoothly*.) Therefore *zoot* is the root of the word *zoong* ya get me?

CHELSEA mimics him, putting on a deep voice and smoking her imaginary zoot.

CHELSEA. *Ohh. I'm bunning a zoot, man.*

CAIN (*laughs*). Yeah – just like that – alright, now keep bunning your zoot.

She reaches for CAIN's actual zoot resting behind his ear. He moves back to dodge her.

Your zoot – not mine.

CHELSEA giggles, enjoying the playful mushy moment. She continues to smoke her zoot.

CHELSEA (*deep voice*). *My bad my bad.*

CAIN. Now tell me how it starts to make you feel.

She takes another long pull on her imaginary zoot, then crosses her eyes and leans to the side.

CHELSEA. *Ahh bruv, I feel mash-up innit.*

CAIN (*laughing*). Okay – well there is a term for that.

CHELSEA. *And what's that bruv?*

CAIN. *Zoonged* out.

CHELSEA. Okay okay – I get it now.

CAIN. So you understand now? Zoot… zoonged out… zoongness.

CHELSEA (*darlingly*). Yeah.

CAIN. So next time you see Fred having a conversation with the curtains in your living room at four o'clock in the morning you can say, 'Oi, that's some *zoongness* right there, Fred.'

CHELSEA *practises*.

CHELSEA. *Oi, that's some zoongness you just did right there, Dad.*

CAIN. Yeah you got it. Those are the main ones 'cause there's more, there's like *zoong-aleng-along* which means just move – be on your way. There's *zoongladite* – there's loads.

CHELSEA (*laughs*). You're funny today.

CAIN. I missed you.

He kisses her.

You know you're gonna be my wife innit.

Come, let's go upstairs.

CHELSEA. Not now.

CAIN (*rolls his head*). Ahhh.

CHELSEA. What's that for? I wanna speak with you.

CAIN. You know how hard I've been waiting for this?

CHELSEA. I can't now anyway.

CAIN. Why not? Are you on your period? Look, I don't care.

If you can walk through mud you can fuck through blood.

CHELSEA. CAIN!

CAIN (*smiling*). Strawberry milkshake –

CHELSEA (*wagging her head in disgust*). Cain, that's nasty. [Why would you say that?] (*Goes to leave.*)

CAIN. [I was joking, I was joking.]

> Cool your foot, just… Oi!

CHELSEA. No, Cain, you just speak without thinking sometimes!

CAIN (*smiling*). It was a joke.

CHELSEA. Well it's not funny!

CAIN. Okay! Cool, just – relax. You're all switching like I said it five times, I was joking.

> CHELSEA *remains standing*.

CHELSEA. It's getting late, I gotta go.

CAIN. Oh, she's gotta go.

CHELSEA. 'Cause you can't be serious.

CAIN. You didn't even come to visit me in prison and now you've gotta go. Suddenly you've got all these things to do right away.

CHELSEA. Some of us have a job! Not all of us can afford to sit on the wall all day every day talking about nothing and doing nothing with your life!

> *Pause*.

CAIN. So that's how you feel.

> CAIN *gets up to leave*.

CHELSEA. No, Cain, wait… you know I didn't mean it like that.

CAIN. I did a year in a cell for you. And I know, you say it was my fault because I overreacted but end of the day *I* was looking out for *you*!

CHELSEA. Cain…

CAIN. But nothing I do meets your standards, even when I'm protecting you.

CHELSEA. I appreciate you looking out for me but…

CAIN. When I was locked up all I was thinking of was you. When I was pushing weights my main drive was what you were gonna think about my body when you saw it. I'd say to myself 'she better still be there when I get back.' Least you can do is have my back like I had yours! I had yours!

Pause.

She stares at him.

CHELSEA. I hate seeing you like this. You've got flesh in your veins. See. That's how you get yourself worked up and do things you'll regret. Cain, I do wanna be with you. But. Not if it's gonna be anything like how it was before. I can't have that on my chest.

CAIN. I ain't even the same like I was before though. That's what I'm trying to tell you...

CHELSEA *gives* CAIN *a look.*

You don't believe me?

CHELSEA. No, it's just... I've heard that before. I don't wanna be going back on myself...

CAIN. On a real – I've got plans. It's a lot, and you'll start seeing – Watch. Stick around long enough and some of this good fortune might rub off on you... and I ain't just saying this but Chelsea you... you make me better. Not many people have the power to change me, not like that – that's why I like you how I do, you make me check myself. That's why you're my girl.

He kisses her.

CHELSEA. But you gotta fix up.

She kisses him.

Fix. Up.

CAIN. Uhm.

CHELSEA. Get a good job.

CAIN. –

CHELSEA. Get an education – can you do that?

CAIN. We'll see.

CHELSEA. Can you do that??

CAIN. Don't ask me no questions and I won't tell you no lies.

CHELSEA. Seriously. Hand out some CVs.

CAIN. Yeah, I might staple my prison-release form to the back page.

CHELSEA. Don't. Don't do that okay?

CAIN. You gonna help me then?

CHELSEA. Of course.

CAIN*'s tag begins to flash and beep.*

CAIN (*hastily*). Shit. I broke my curfew, they're gonna call my house phone.

CHELSEA. It beeps?

CAIN (*rushing off*). Gotta go.

CHELSEA. I'll speak to you tomorrow.

CAIN. You ain't coming?

Come.

They go.

Scene Three

The next day, the sun is shining. OBI *sits on the wall. Musing and writing.*

OBI (*reading and writing*). I hate wanting you
    That makes me sick
    When I see you... when. I. see. youuuu
    My life is shit
    So I'll pretend
    Like things are cool
    'Cause when I don't... 'cause when I don't...
    I'm vulnerable
    You're beautiful.

    CHELSEA *arrives*.

CHELSEA. Obi.

    He tenses, keeps his eyes on the page.

    Obi.

    Do you mind raising your head out of your book for one
    moment?

OBI. Sup?

    I haven't seen Cain if that's what you're...

CHELSEA. I came to see you actually.

OBI. –

CHELSEA. Yes, you.

OBI. Okay.

    What about?

CHELSEA. I'll ask the questions thank you. As you know
    Cain's back.

OBI. Yes indeed.

CHELSEA. What are you lot planning?

OBI (*baffled*). Planning...

CHELSEA. And don't play dumb because I can sense trouble from a mile away.

OBI. What?

CHELSEA. Look, let me break it down for you. You see me yeah? I'm not dumb, you can't lie to me, I deal with guys like you at the youth club eh-ver-y day it's a minor.

OBI. What?

CHELSEA. You see Cain? That's my man. And I know when he's hiding something. So just tell me, what are you making him do this time?

OBI. What am *I* making him do?

CHELSEA. Yes you, you're a bad influence on him, I know you're trying to drag him down with you.

OBI. Me?

CHELSEA. Don't try and act all innocent because I was there that time when you dared him to steal the pizza-delivery man's moped...

OBI. What?

CHELSEA. ...and now they don't deliver pizza here any more all because of Obi.

OBI. We were fifteen.

CHELSEA. I don't care how old you were, you've got some hold on him and I don't like it, making him do bad things – I know it's you.

OBI. ME?

CHELSEA. *Da dark lord with the sharp sword...*

OBI (*gathering her assumption*). Okay.

CHELSEA. I know what the sharp sword is ya know.

OBI. I don't do that any more.

I'm the one that's been trying to get him to cool his head.

CHELSEA. Whatever. I'm gonna find out what this plan is that you lot got going.

OBI. I'll just tell you straight.

Pause.

CHELSEA. Go on then.

OBI. They're gonna go and wet up Delvin.

CHELSEA. Shut up.

OBI. I'm serious, they're talking about killing him.

CHELSEA. Obi. Get a life. Normal people don't joke about them things do they? Anyway I know Cain wouldn't do that sooo… (*Goes to leave.*)

OBI *goes back to his writing.*

OBI. Okay, don't believe me.

She stops. Turns around.

CHELSEA. You're always writing something innit.

What are you writing?

OBI. –

CHELSEA. I bet it's all, 'fuck bitch shit ass nigga motherfucker blood'. You lot need to learn how to write proper sentences.

OBI (*laughs*). That's cute.

CHELSEA. What are you writing?

OBI. Chelsea wants to know what Obi's writing.

CHELSEA (*kisses her teeth*). Forget it then.

OBI. Nar I'll show you but I just wanna make sure you're… ready. 'Tis some deep deep shit that might fly overhead.

CHELSEA. Uh. Excuse me, but I got an A-star in English Lit so I'll be the judge of that thank you.

She sits close beside him.

OBI. It's my book of poetry.

CHELSEA. Wait wait, *you* write poems?

OBI. Yes.

CHELSEA. Oh my days. But you're a waste-man though?

OBI. What?! How am I a waste-man?

CHELSEA (*laughing*). Every guy on this estate is a waste-man.

OBI. What about your dad?

CHELSEA. A waste-man is a waste-man is a waste-man.

They laugh together.

OBI. Oh but Cain is the biggest waste-man though, who comes out of prison, has a beautiful girl who *waited* for them and doesn't go to see her first thing?

He realises what he's said. Awkward moment.

SO the poem...

CHELSEA. Yeah the...

OBI. Now, this one's not finished yet, it's more like... (*Clocks her watching him.*) what?

CHELSEA. What?

OBI. Why you looking at me like that?

CHELSEA. I ain't looking at you no-how carry on.

OBI. Okay.

So. It's more of a game than a poem – (*Indicating and sharing the page.*) that's you and that's me.

CHELSEA. I'm reading?

OBI. It's a two-person poem.

CHELSEA. There's four lines.

OBI. After that, we improvise.

CHELSEA. Improvise?

Bye, Obi... (*Goes to leave.*)

OBI. You didn't strike me as one to chicken out, being an A-star student and all dat.

Pause.

CHELSEA *(feistily)*. You think you're bad innit?

OBI. [I don't think I'm bad.]

CHELSEA. [You think you're heavy.] Well, you've just met your match – Read it.

OBI. This isn't a compe–

CHELSEA. / Read it.

He reads.

OBI. I like you. It's a lot.

CHELSEA. How much?

OBI. So much that if I should write it down, and set the note in a bottle, and this bottle should fall, through the air, fifteen storeys down to my estate compound, the ground would split in two, sending a gaping crack from here, through Mansa Musa's mansion in Timbuktu and through the rearing volcano behind it, dividing it down the middle, imploring it to weep magma from the earth's crust, commissioning burning lava onto the town, spreading and refilling the crack that cast the city asunder, only to be pacified upon arrival at the ocean, after vanishing everything in its wake.

He shuts the book.

I liked you straight away, like when I put my iPod on shuffle and Michael Jackson came on.

CHELSEA *(laughing)*. You can say that?

OBI. You can say whatever.

CHELSEA. Okay... mmm, wait... I can't think.

OBI. I need you like... internet.

CHELSEA. I need you like... hands to a magician.

OBI. I need you like firemen need a raise.

CHELSEA. I need you like a trolly at Safeways.

OBI. I need you like ice cream on Sundays.

CHELSEA. I need more ways to describe all the ways that
I need you. It's a lot.

OBI. How much?

CHELSEA. So much that when I hear your sweet voice my
eardrums burst, scarcely do I see you when I'm reminded why
we have eyes, I'd wait here forever if I heard you were
coming, even when I kiss you I already miss you – a little too
much, you stay on my mind like cranium, I could watch you
for all the heat in the sun, when I look away from you there's a
rainbow in my eyes as if I've been staring at the light for too
long, I need you but I can't reveal it, ten is the square root of
how many beats my heart skips whenever we have to conceal
it… nothing else matters, all else fades to black, when I smell
you my nose breaks – just like that, when you touch me my
bones are reduced to powder, and should any gymnast use this
powder for their hands, any mother apply this powder to their
baby's bottom, any… Reggie, put this powder up his nose,
each and every gymnast, baby and Reggie, would have the
rhythm in their heartbeat, cease.

OBI. Rah.

Erm… you make my palms sweat, like I'm holding one-
pound coins.

CHELSEA. You make me happy like when the Oyster machine
on the bus ain't working.

OBI. Not being with you pisses me off like the zip on my
jacket.

CHELSEA. Not being with you pisses me off like when my
little toe hits the corner of the doorframe.

OBI. Not being with you pisses me off like the space between
my bed and the wall when I'm trying to have sex.

CHELSEA. I love you – (*Long beat.*) to the sound of birds at
2.55 a.m.

OBI. I love you big like the sky above you.

CHELSEA. I love you deep through the ground beneath you, to the other side.

OBI. I love you from here to the sun.

    In slow motion.

CHELSEA. And back?

OBI. While walking backwards.

    On my hands.

    Instinctively, OBI *kisses her.*

    They kiss.

    She pushes him away.

CHELSEA. What are you doing?

OBI. Ah?

    She kisses him.

    They kiss, longer.

    She pushes him away.

    She goes to leave.

    Wait wait…

    She waits.

    He has no words.

    She leaves.

MYLES. *'Cause she understaaaaands me.*

    Scarcely does CHELSEA *exit than* MYLES *enters speaking on the phone in his R&B voice.*

    OBI *and* MYLES *bump fists.* MYLES *gestures 'good times on a sunny Saturday afternoon' towards him.* OBI *donates a smile.*

    MYLES *props his foot up on the wall and spit-cleans the front of his new Nike Airs. In his hand is a* Rewind *magazine; a monthly issue about UK grime and hip-hop artists.*

(*To phone*.) She understands *me*, baby girl – me. 'Cause, baby, I'm twenty years young, and you know it. You haven't even got a belly button, 'cause you understaaaaands me – God just made you like that. Buff. And then after, beep beep beeeeeeeeeeeep. And I'm dead... (*Sadly*.) Unfortunately I'm dead. The end. Thank you. I'm kinda deep, you're right. Nar, wrote it myself – Inspired by last night's *events*. I know... I bet your man can't do it like me can he? WHAT?

MYLES *grabs his crotch*.

Look, it might be small but so is dynamite.

MYLES, *while having his phone conversation, opens up a page in the* Rewind *magazine and urges* OBI *to read it*.

(*To phone*.) Exackly – so therefore it is *not* the size of the boat it's the motion of the ocean.

OBI. Only mans with small dicks say that shit.

OBI *reads the article*.

Oh seen. This is Delvin.

MYLES (*to phone*). See it was nice when you done that but you missed a spot.

OBI. MC Delvin. That's a shit name though.

MYLES (*to phone*). Were we playing dodge ball? No. So then how are you gonna give me head and then dodge the balls?

OBI (*reading the magazine aloud*). 'MC Delvin has fast-tracked into the centre of the UK grime scene by teaming up with the Roll Deep Squad' – not bad. 'His mix-tape *Cold as Ice* is hosted by WILEY and is flooding the streets from the first of August.'

Listen to that, man. Certified.

CAIN *arrives*.

CAIN. Obi One, I see the true dark lord's come out to play.

MYLES (*to phone, rushing off*). I'll chat to you later, babe. (*To* CAIN.) Oi, *I'm* the dark lord today, b.

CAIN (*to* OBI). I'm letting him hold the sword, only until the rightful lord returns of course. Look at him, happy as a baby in a driver seat.

MYLES. You ready?

CAIN. Are *you* ready?

MYLES. I was born ready.

CAIN. Well let's do this.

OBI. What's going on?

MYLES (*ignoring* OBI). Do I look hench? I wore like three jumpers, b.

CAIN. You're cool.

OBI. Where are youse lot going?

MYLES. We're gonna go see a boy about a bank.

CAIN (*indicates to the magazine*). Sort things out wit' boy wonder. We're gonna delve into Delvin's world.

MYLES. Might have to SMASH him up if he tries to act fresh. True-say he's Wiley's protégé now. He might think he's too hot. See that's why – that's why I got *this*, call me the dark lord from now on, nuffin else.

MYLES *raises his jumpers right up to his chest.*

OBI. You're just showing me the dry skin on your belly.

MYLES. See, I hide that so good – (*To* CAIN.) he can't even see it – the sharp sword is down there, patiently waiting his turn.

OBI. The whole point of having it on your waist is for *easy* access.

MYLES. I'm Billy the Kid I'll shank him before he blinks. [I'm a digidigidigidigi-dan.]

MYLES *gets excited and starts to dance.*

CAIN. Gonna handle business.

MYLES (*still dancing*). Handle business, I like that.

> *Businessmen* you get me?

> Yeah – I see it now.

> This is a new beginning.

CAIN. Let's go.

MYLES. Let's-go-let's-go-let's-go.

> MYLES *dances off, adrenalised*.

> CAIN *turns to* OBI.

CAIN. Come we do this, man.

OBI. Nar, I'll stay here.

CAIN. Women and children stay home, soldiers go out to battle.

OBI. But you're a rebel without a cause.

CAIN. I do have a cause.

OBI. When police catch you and ask you why you did it you'll be scratching you head, bruv.

CAIN. But I do have a cause though.

OBI. Go on.

CAIN. My cause is to protect the estate from pricks like Delvin.

OBI. Stupid, that's stupid. When are you gonna get fed up of proving yourself?

CAIN (*smiling*). *When are you gonna get fed up of proving yourself*. Pussy.

OBI. Yes. (*Sotto*.) Turn it into a joke.

CAIN (*leaving*). I'm gone!

> Oh, did you see – ? (*Points to* CHELSEA*'s balcony*.)

OBI. Nah.

CAIN. No?

> OBI *shakes his head*.

CAIN. Good, 'cause she said she was gonna go chat to you about something, listen, if she asks you, tell her you / don't know nothing about nothing.

OBI. / don't know nothing about nothing.

CAIN. Exactly. Just like old times.

OBI. Uhm.

CAIN *exits*.

Scene Four

Moments later. MYLES *and* CAIN *walk on the street.*

MYLES *flicks out the knife and brandishes it.*

MYLES. Man, this thing's giving me confidence, b.

CAIN. Put it away.

MYLES. *The silver Stanley makes you feel manly.* It feels like an extension to my hand. I feel like if anyone came and tried anything I'd just – (*Demonstrates stabbing.*) Even if police come I wouldn't run ya know. I ain't running from no police. I'm gully. I don't run, I'll be like 'What? What you say, b? Just coz you're police you think I won't wet you up? What...' (*Demonstrates more stabbing.*) – swear down. What would you do if a man came here now and goes 'gimme your stuff bloood', what would you do, would you run?

CAIN. I'd tell him to suck his mum.

MYLES. BRAP! Then what?

CAIN. Then I send him on his way.

MYLES (*playing with the knife*). That's all? Man, if that was me I'll end it right there, b, I'll have him laying there right where he stood.

CAIN. Pass it. The knife. I'll hold it.

MYLES (*whining*). Why, man?

CAIN. I don't trust you with it.

MYLES. B, you never let me do nuffin, man, I got it all under control.

CHELSEA. Cain.

> CHELSEA *arrives, frightening* MYLES*, who jumps, lands badly on his ankle, drops the knife and takes a Karate Kid stance*.

> CAIN *picks up the knife and pockets it*.

MYLES. Chelsea, man! It's dangerous to creep up on bad mans like that. You could get hurt.

CAIN. Myles.

MYLES (*walking off, under his breath*). Making mans twist his ankle and dat...

> MYLES *exits*.

CAIN. I know what you're gonna say.

CHELSEA. If you do this, Cain, if you go through with this. It's over. We're finished.

> I can't stand beside you while you do this. This time I know it's all on you, nobody's making you do anything.

CAIN. The boy's been driving around *my* estate like he's running tings, you want me to just [fucking sit there...]

CHELSEA. [He hasn't done anything to you.]

CAIN (*leaving*)....He's gonna humble hisself, today, even if it's by force. Myles is waiting for me.

CHELSEA. So you're going yeah?

CAIN. What do you expect me to do! Yes! I'm going! Yes! See, that's why I don't tell you anything, you just get me vexed...

CHELSEA. You know what your problem is? You can't see what you're doing to yourself, you never think ahead do you? Cain, you're not a little boy any more...

CAIN. DON'T get all fucking youth-worker on me, I ain't one of your kids y'understand?

CHELSEA (*leaving*). Fine, go. We want different things anyway.

CAIN (*leaving*). While your mum was tucking you into bed at night, I was getting beat out of my sleep by my dad…

CHELSEA (*leaving*). We know that story, Cain.

CAIN.…So don't speak to me about being a little boy. Don't fucking ever call me a little boy ever again!

CHELSEA. Fine!

CAIN (*leaving*). I'M A BIG MAN! You always come with all your advice yeah but it's easy for you to say 'don't do this, don't do that'.

CHELSEA (*leaving*). Yep.

CAIN. We *do* want different things, you're right, we do. 'Cause *you* want me to be like you, I can't do that for you.

CHELSEA. That's not what I want.

CAIN. This is what I know. I can't be like you. I'm a bad breed. I can only be me.

CHELSEA *exits*.

Scene Five

Later that day. CAIN *staggers onto the estate.* MYLES *has his arm around* CAIN, *helping him to walk.*

MYLES (*distressed*). OBI!

OI, OBI! THEY GOT CAIN, MAN! OBI! OBI!

CAIN (*in pain*). Obi…

OBI *rushes onto the scene and immediately attends to* CAIN, *who is now slumped against the wall.*

OBI. Fuck. What happened?

MYLES (*pacing up and down*). They got him, b. We gotta go back there, b! We gotta go get 'em, b. They're gonna get it, b. They ain't gonna get away with this, b. We gotta kill 'em all, b.

CAIN. Obi One, come closer… closer. Tell Chelsea… Tell Chelsea… I love her.

MYLES. Beep beep beeeeeeeeeeeep.

MYLES *and* CAIN *crash into laugher.* MYLES *rolls around on the floor.*

Hahaha you believed us!

OBI. You dickheads.

CAIN. You see his face?

OBI. Get off me.

CAIN. He was all about to cry.

MYLES. Innit though. *Cain, don't go.* At least it made him put down his book for once.

MYLES *picks up* OBI's *book.*

OBI. Pass it.

MYLES. Smells like fresh ink, what you been writing?

He throws it over to CAIN.

CAIN. Ooh nice throw.

MYLES. Nice catch.

OBI. Pass my book!

MYLES. Rah, getting angry.

CAIN. He's upset.

> CAIN *throws it over to* MYLES, *they throw it back and forth, teasing* OBI, *playing Piggy in the Middle*.

OBI. I swear to God if you don't give me my book I'm gonna start throwing blows.

CAIN *and* MYLES. Ooh.

OBI. I'm fucking serious.

MYLES. Don't cry, b, here, you can have your book.

> *Before handing it to him,* MYLES *slyly rips out a page.*

> *Enter* REGGIE.

REGGIE. I heard you calling.

MYLES. Is your name Obi?

CAIN (*to* OBI). Obi One.

REGGIE. Fair enough.

> But don't you owe me something.

OBI. You lot are dickheads.

> MYLES *pulls out some notes. Tens and twenties.* REGGIE's *eyes are candied instantly.*

REGGIE. Fuck-in'-hell-Sam-u-el, who did you kill for that?

CAIN. You give me bare joke. You should've seen your face.

MYLES. Have you got change of a ten?

OBI. Come off me.

REGGIE. Yes I do – (*Goes through his pockets.*)

CAIN. We was joking, bruv.

REGGIE. Wait a minute, what do you mean change of a ten, you owe me ten!

OBI. Don't joke about them things.

MYLES. Listen I'll give you a tenner for now but you make sure you bring me back my change.

REGGIE (*indignantly*). Bullshit.

MYLES. I'm joking, man, chill chill, it's all yours, b.

MYLES *crushes the tenner into a ball and flicks it at* REGGIE. REGGIE *catches it, unfolds it, and holds it to the sky to examine it.*

CAIN. Don't spend it all on crack.

REGGIE. I won't.

MYLES (*singing*). *Ah don't believe youuuu.*

Hi my name's Obi and I'm a writer-holic, hahaha… He's gonna be an author like Harry Potter.

OBI. Dunce.

CAIN. Obi One. Where you been, soldier?

OBI. In my yard.

MYLES. What were you doing 'in your yard'?

OBI. What's it to you?

MYLES (*to* CAIN). That means he was wanking.

OBI. Shut up.

MYLES. Look at his face – all flushed, he just ejaculated like two minutes ago – let me see your hand.

MYLES *and* CAIN *laugh.*

REGGIE *laughs with them, a little too much. The boys stop and look at him.*

REGGIE. Oh, Myles, you crack me up. Get it? *Crack* me up? (*Laugh-coughs at his own joke.*)

No really, I'm glad you're satisfied, we'll do business again soon – the trainers really suit you.

MYLES. Shut up.

REGGIE. I'm not being funny, lads, but I really can get a hold of things.

MYLES. Just go already.

REGGIE. And if any of you are interested in buying a gun, a real one, I won't even ask you why you need it – it's already sorted.

I'm your guy.

REGGIE *bows and then exits. The boys watch him leave with the ten-pound note clutched in his hand.*

MYLES *turns to* OBI.

MYLES. Bruv, you missed out, man.

You missed out BIG.

OBI. Go on.

MYLES. I ain't even gonna lie – you missed out, b.

OBI (*eagerly*). What happened?

MYLES. You – missed – OUT.

OBI. Tell it then.

MYLES. What happens off the block stays off the block – I wish I could tell it – but I can't. I wish I could show you 'cause I was gonna film it for my documentary but I didn't wanna have evidence that could be used against me on my phone. Hard evidence like – exhibit-A-type evidence.

OBI. Cain, what happened?

CAIN. Well /

MYLES. / Let me tell it, man, damn. Listen, you're lucky I'm even telling but – we must have bowled into Woodberry Downs Estate. All the mandem got shook. I must have asked them '*Where's Delvin that pussole Turkish boy?*', but we already knew where he was really – I just wanted to see if they would lie – 'cause if they lied it would have turned into a bloodbath, get me? The blood would've run the streets

knee-high to my horse, get me? I would have started
smashing pumpkins 'cause when I'm vexed like dat...

OBI. Go on go on go on.

MYLES. I sees him now. And he sees me yeah – with Cain.
And. I must have pulled him to the side and I was kinda
gentle at first but then I SLAPPED him right in his mouth.
And I said '*Your green mouth is too big*' – he started trying
to apologise and shit and I said to him '*b, you know that
snitches get stitches innit, snitches get stitches blooood!*'

MYLES *pauses to think.*

OBI. Then what?

MYLES (*clearly creating the story as he goes along*). Then
what, then obviously after that I I I... put my foot down – on
his neck – yeah.

(*Demonstrating.*) Like this. And he was shitting his pants.

I said 'B, B! Where's my money, b?' He said –

– *Myles, I don't know what you're talking about.*'

– '*B! Where's my money?*'

– '*I swear on my mum's grave I don't know...*'

– '*Gonna ask you one more time, b, and don't gimme
information about your mum's grave 'cause I ain't even
concern. Where's-my-monies you Turkish delight?*'

He didn't even answer me so – so I I... I just SHANKED
him up. Stabbed him and he died.

OBI. Shut up, man!

MYLES. [I swear down!]

OBI. [You chat rubbish.]

MYLES. Alright don't believe me, you'll see it on *Crimewatch*.

OBI. Cain, what happened?

MYLES. Cain, tell him.

CAIN. We went down there, I phoned him, he came out of his yard and we spoke.

MYLES. Why you killing it for? He believed me as well.

OBI. Go on.

CAIN. He says /

MYLES. / He says he ain't like that no more and that if he could take it back he would and that prison changed him. Then he just dropped us some dough – and a CD.

OBI. How much?

MYLES. Just one CD with like – eight tracks on it.

OBI. How much money you *zoonger*?

MYLES. Oh – I got ninety pound.

OBI. What about you, Cain.

CAIN. Don't worry.

MYLES. Cain got about t…

CAIN *shoots* MYLES *a look*.

…I was joking, man, I wasn't gonna say.

Silent operation innit.

MYLES *mimes the words 'two hundred pounds' to* OBI *without* CAIN *seeing*.

OBI. He's not gonna shot for your uncle then?

MYLES. He ain't gonna have enough time 'cause he's bringing out a mix-tape – *Cold as Ice* it's called – it's got all the baddest UK grime artist featuring on it. When that drops he'll be busy doing shows and that, but Cain said we should just squash it, we're even now.

Oh and Chelsea came.

OBI. Chelsea?

MYLES. Yeah, man, she almost ruined it. What did she have to tell you that was so urgent anyhow?

CAIN. Nothing.

MYLES. Hear that, Obi? 'Nothing', that's exactly the same thing what you got in your pocket. The jealousy's infecting you innit?

OBI. Nah – don't care.

MYLES. Don't lie, don't lie you got jealous fever 'cause we got money and you got dust.

OBI. Couldn't care less.

MYLES, *during this speech, puts his hand down his trousers and begins to scratch at his crotch. First gently, then gradually more aggressively, as he proceeds:*

MYLES. Yeah, b – you can say that but we know the truth – we know. Deep down inside you want some of that money. While you're all tryina be some *model A-one citizen* – trying to act all high-horsified, thinking you're better than us with your poetry and deep slanguage and your flipping miniature submarine toys hanging from your ceiling, we're out there getting money – showing face – making plans and shaking hands, letting mans know we're for real – it's not for play – this ain't a playground, b, this ain't a game, this ain't Connect 4. We growed up, we sip coffee in the staffroom now. Businessmen ya'getz. And you're in your yard wanking to your own poetry books. I don't have to wank, rude boi, I don't have to, 'cause I get the pum-pum frequently – from now on you call me '*the pumster… pumplexer* MYLES' – yeah – sounds nice innit – I know – 'cause, I made it up – what. And don't try and chat to me about Channy. I did bang her AND WHAT? SO? At least she can bang. *Your* girls are like pillows they're only good for head.

They watch MYLES *in disbelief as he claws at his crotch.*

OBI (*in disgust*). Er, bruv!

CAIN. What are you doing?

OBI. You're nasty, man.

CAIN. You need to stop that from now, rude boi.

MYLES (*patting and slapping at his crotch*). Fuck.

It's itching.

OBI. Go to your yard and do that, bruv.

MYLES. Nar you don't understand this is fire, b – like it's burning, b!

CAIN. I don't care I don't wanna see that nastiness.

MYLES. Ah, it's burning! Stop looking at me like dat!

OBI. SEE! I told you! What did I tell you?

MYLES. What?

OBI. What did I tell you? I knew it.

You didn't use a condom did you? You got STI.

MYLES. Shut up.

CAIN. Did you use it?

MYLES. Why am I gonna use it when she's on the pill?

OBI. Are your ears for fashion? I told you the pill don't stop diseases!

S to the T to the I, rude boi.

MYLES. I ain't got no S to the T to the I, man.

OBI. I bet you any money you've got STI.

CAIN. You probably do, Myles.

MYLES. Shit.

OBI. Told you!

MYLES. But *how*?

OBI. Now your dick's gonna look like a Peperami. You better get your little willy checked up before it shrivels up.

MYLES. I beg one of you, come to the clinic with me.

The boys say nothing.

Please, man.

Cain?

CAIN. Okay. I'll go.

MYLES. Safe, man.

MYLES *scurries off, walking with his knees turned in –* CAIN *stands to leave.*

OBI. You gave Delvin a slap on the wrist today.

CAIN. Ptshh…

OBI. Change of heart?

CAIN. It's *dat* girl innit. (*Gestures towards* CHELSEA*'s window.*) That girl makes me so angry it's unhealthy.

I *had* to let him go – I couldn't fuck him up if I tried 'cause all I could hear was Chelsea's voice in the back of my head nagging me.

One of the first lessons I learnt was to always 'MOB' – MOB. Always put Money Over Bitches, but I bombed it today, I… BOM'ed.

OBI. You did the right thing.

CAIN. But don't get it twisted I'm still top of the food chain, still a badman, still a carnivorous predator out here.

OBI. I have no doubt in my mind that you are all of those things.

CAIN. She's on my case about getting a job, fixing up.

OBI. And?

CAIN. And I ain't doing shit… for now.

I told her I'll think about it.

Even if I *was* to do it… I'd need more time to… (*Searches.*)

OBI. Ease into it?

CAIN. Exactly. Ease into it.

Then, I'd probably get fired for stealing out of the till.

OBI. They probably *would* fire you for that – Happily. That's why you shouldn't do that, bro.

Pause.

CAIN (*inside*). Ahhh.

I feel small, man.

OBI. How?

CAIN. I feel small. Chelsea's made me feel small. And you, you're making me feel small right now – talking to me.

OBI. Sorry.

CAIN. It's cool. You're not doing it on purpose, it's just how *I* feel.

CAIN *pulls a wad of cash from his pockets and splits it. He holds it out to* OBI.

OBI. What's this?

CAIN *forces it into* OBI*'s palm.*

CAIN. Obi One.

He exits.

OBI. When the estate ain't loud enough I can still hear the voices in my head.

CHELSEA *comes out onto her balcony.*

CHELSEA. Obi One.

OBI. Chels.

Pause.

CHELSEA. That poem was all right.

OBI *nods.*

'Cept for your parts. Kinda dry.

OBI (*laughs*). Oh really.

CHELSEA. Nar.

I think you're a wicked poet. And... nar go on, you were gonna say something.

OBI. Thank you. So are you.

CHELSEA. Can you read me another one?

OBI. Chelsea, I would love to read you something I wrote this afternoon.

He flips open his book.

That's weird I... it's not here. No but... ah, the page must've... it must've dropped out.

CHELSEA. Or maybe you didn't write it.

OBI (*panicking, combing the area*). It's gotta be in my room or something, on the floor.

CHELSEA. I'll come down.

She leaves the balcony.

OBI (*shouting up to her window*). No. I'll... I'll go get it!

OBI *leaves, tracing his steps.*

Moments later, CAIN *arrives.* CHELSEA *descends and is surprised to find* CAIN *there.*

Pause.

CAIN. Know what, I missed my estate. I missed it, more than the people in it. Just the whole structure of it. Ninety-three families crammed in like sardines in a can, you can't even look out your window without looking into someone else's, everyone knows everyone's business – it's kinda like prison. It's a lot. It's a lot like a prison.

Come, sit. Come...

Are you deaf?

CHELSEA. What do you want?

CAIN. Let me rap to you for a second.

CHELSEA (*leaving*). I don't have time for this.

CAIN. Chelsea, I beg, I'm not gonna ask you again...

CHELSEA. It's your fault, I told you not to go and you went!

CAIN. Well really, it didn't matter if I went or not, you already had your mind made up, Chels.

Firstly. If you wasn't feeling me any more you should've said. Secondly...

CHELSEA. What?!

CAIN. ...secondly, lemme finish, this estate is too small fucking tiny, secrets yeah, this ain't the place for secrets.

He pulls a rumpled sheet out of his pocket.

It's proper deep. Look, Myles ripped this out of Obi's book – 'cause Obi's got this book like, he's a poet now, sure you already know this, but listen, there's one... there's this lyric you gotta read 'cause...

He hands the poem to CHELSEA.

CHELSEA. Cain...

CAIN. ...Myles dropped it in my palm and was like 'yo read it read it read it' and man got past the first few lines and like – actually know what, lemme stop talking innit, just read the ting.

CHELSEA *looks at it.*

Don't read it in your head, girl, read it out loud, it's a good poem.

That's an understatement actually, the poem's sick, I gotta give the boy his props, he's mad talented. (*Gestures for her to read it.*)

CHELSEA. Cain. Seriously...

CAIN. Nah, it don't start with '*Cain seriously*', read from the paper in your hand. Start again.

CHELSEA. I'm not reading this.

CAIN. Read it from the top.

With the title and all-dat.

I wanna get the full effect.

Beat.

CHELSEA *scrunches the paper into a ball and goes to put it in the bin.*

(*Going after her.*) Oh now, Chels, what would you go and do that for ah?

CHELSEA. [Come out of my way! Move, man.]

CAIN. [That's nuff silly, Chelsea. Get it out the bin.]

CHELSEA. No.

CAIN *grabs her hand and forces it onto his waist. She can feel the knife.*

CHELSEA *picks the paper out of the bin.*

CAIN. Now go sit over there.

CHELSEA, *now breaking down, goes and sits on the wall. She covers her face, crying.*

You're leaking, why you leaking for? Get over yourself, blood. You chose to do what you did.

CHELSEA (*crying*). You gonna stab me over what?! [Are you serious? Fucking hell, man.]

CAIN. [Ay ay who said anything about stabbing? I didn't say that.] Did you hear me say that? You got a wild imagination. Like Obi.

Read.

CHELSEA. He can't see you, the way I see you
He doesn't understand
He never holds your hand
You see the clouds as cracks in the sky
He sees the sky through the cracks in the clouds

CAIN. You're rushing through it. Don't do that.

Run the last line again.

CHELSEA. You see the clouds as cracks in the sky
/ He sees the sky through the cracks in the clouds.

CAIN. / He sees the sky through the cracks in the clouds.

Sick. Go on.

CHELSEA. You've never seen a farm – I've never seen a forest
– We've never seen even a beach.
On Carnival Sunday, you ran through the crowd to stroke the
police horse in the street.

CAIN (*stifles laughter*). That was jokes.

CHELSEA. We both want more
But drew the short straw
Having grown within these estate walls.
But when we kissed like –

CAIN. Uhm.

CHELSEA. Chelsea, you made me wanna take a little trip like –

CAIN. Sick.

CHELSEA. To the moon,
So I could bring you back a bit of it.

CAIN. Of the moon, fam!

CHELSEA. You're the best thing in Pembury Estate
And not being with you
Pisses me off
Like the shirt-tag scratching on my nape – (*Folds the poem.*)

CAIN. What's a nape?

CHELSEA. The back of your neck.

CAIN. Oh.

Sick.

My boy and my girl.

That's… that's some poetic shit.

Phone him, tell him to come down and all three of us can
speak on it.

CHELSEA. Cain, it was just a kiss. That's all that happened, it
just happened.

CAIN. Izit?

CHELSEA. Yeah.

CAIN. So then why's man chatting about bringing you back a piece of the moon? Real talk.

CHELSEA (*leaving*). I'm sorry I kissed your friend.

CAIN. Where the fuck you think you're going? I said CALL HIM, we'll sort this ting.

CHELSEA. Move out my way.

CAIN. Gimme your phone.

CHELSEA. What's your problem, leave me alone. Get... get off my arm or I'm gonna scream!

She screams.

In sudden hysteria, CAIN *loses it. Blistering with rage, he slams her to the floor. She struggles but he kneels over her, pinning her firmly to the ground.*

Her phone slips out of her pocket.

CAIN. Oi stop... stay still! Are you trying to bite me? Are you... DON'T SCRATCH ME!

CHELSEA. Then get off me!

CAIN. Listen you're kinda strong...

CHELSEA. [Get off me! Help!]

CAIN. ...but I'm stronger, nobody's gonna help you – this is my estate, they help me here.

He picks up her phone. He tries to phone OBI *but the call doesn't go through.*

He stands on the wall, shouting up the estate building.

Oi, Obi!

You're a G – a gangster!

'Cause you've been fucking my girl – and I didn't even know.

I thought you was my brother, man, brothers don't do that to each other.

Strike three.

You're dead!

You must think I'm a prick. I'm a prick yeah? I'm a prick innit?

You-don't-value-your-life.

You're dead! You forced my hand, I don't even wanna do this, blood! But you got me this way.

Let me see you on the estate – if I catch you on the block again – I'm gonna kill you.

BOOP! BOOP! BOOP!

And I mean it!

I mean it.

He leaves.

Scene Six

Later that evening, on the street. MYLES *and* REGGIE *enter.* REGGIE *records him on the camera-phone.*

MYLES (*presenting to the camera-phone*). Ay, it's Myles signing on, the twenty-years-young don. Here we are at day two on *Camera-Phone Diaries Volume One: Council Estate of Mind.* As you have seen things have heated up. People have been threatening to die and people have been threatening to steal next people's girls – it's crazy.

I mean who'd have known? Obi, the brother who is always handing out advice is the snakiest man in da grass. It's all real, b, no batteries included and no strings attached, b. The shit has hit the turbine.

I, Myles the most handsome of them all, have somehow found myself in this mix. I might've wetted my beak with the bad water and I've fallen ill with... with... (*Raising the medicine box*.) Chlamydia. It still burns when I pee. Discharge and all that, it's not buff. Doctor says I caught it from Channy, personally I think I caught it from a bicycle seat but whatever – agree to disagree. But just in case it was Channy, I'll make a point at my own expense; if a girl says she's on the pill, go to her house with a glass of water every day and watch her swallow that pill!

Now, I did promise you some juicy visuals, I bet you viewers are thinking, 'What's Myles doing on the road, beyond the estate walls that be's the background so frequent.'

Well, me and Reggie a.k.a. crack-lover are on our way to meet my boy, Obi, who apparently is gonna get utterly destroyed, obliterated and discontinued by another dear friend of mine, Cain – they're about to trade flesh and blood. The plot thickens as the clock tickens… here he is now. (Reggie I need a close-up.)

OBI *approaches*.

So, Obi, how do you feel about this whole… zoongness, if you will?

OBI. What's Reggie doing here?

MYLES. He's my cameraman, I'm paying him one pound a day.

REGGIE *films the whole thing*. MYLES *acts up for the camera*.

OBI. So? What did he say?

MYLES. You heard what he said. We all heard what he said – loud 'n' clear!

OBI. Does he mean it though?

MYLES. You shouldn't have moved to his girl, b.

OBI. DOES HE MEAN IT?

MYLES. He's vexed, b – what you expect? You wet your beak upon her juices.

OBI (*to* REGGIE). Reggie, get that fucking camera out my face!

MYLES (*to* REGGIE). Keep rolling.

OBI. So he means it yeah? He said he's gonna try to kill me, is that what he's on?

MYLES. He read the poem, b.

OBI. FUCK.

MYLES. I know, but listen, Obi, calm down, calm down. Can I be real with you? Listen, wise words. I wouldn't, wanna trade places with you right now. Wouldn't wanna be in your shoes, b. That's it. That's all I'm saying.

OBI. What the fff… why you telling me that for, is that supposed to make me feel better?!

MYLES. Some wise words for you…

OBI. Reggie, I swear if you don't get that camera out of my face…

MYLES. …Sometimes, Cain's all mouth but most of the time, he will certainly FUCK you up. Naturally. And he'll take it too far. I came here to remind you. Lest you forget.

OBI (*sotto*). I gotta protect myself.

MYLES. …Plus, he is well *equipped*, if you know what I'm saying. So basically he is strapped *and* he's stronger than you. What can you do? But these are the cosy situations karma puts you in when you juice others people's tings, b. These things are like wildfire, you lot need to squash it before it gets out of hand.

OBI *glances at* REGGIE. *A thought comes to mind. He sees an opportunity, a way to resolve this thing once and for all.*

B, I ain't even gonna lie, you're kinda dumb though. If you're gonna do something like that don't write about it in your book… /

OBI (*heated*). / Myles, if you ain't got nothing to say that's gonna benefit my situation, then hold your mouth.

MYLES. Can't you see I'm trying to help you?

OBI. Just fuck off, man.

MYLES. Yeah? Cool, that's how you're gonna be yeah?

OBI. You came here to see what I was doing so you can run back and tell him.

MYLES. Don't try and switch it round, b, *you're* the snake.

In a flash of anger, OBI *squares up with* MYLES – *his fingers ball into a fist. He pushes his head against* MYLES', *sending him backwards.*

OBI. Alright, bruv, it's time for you to go.

REGGIE, COME HERE!

MYLES. You wanna calm down… get that flesh out of your blood before you do something stupid /

OBI. / Are you still here? *I'm* done. I'm done with you!

MYLES *takes his camera-phone from* REGGIE. *He exits.*

OBI *watches him go, then regards* REGGIE.

Come here, come here!

OBI *whispers in his ear.*

REGGIE (*eagerly*). Yes yes yes… sorted, mate… sorted… that's fine… when? now? We'll do it now.

OBI (*a loud whisper*). Listen first.

OBI *whispers more into* REGGIE's *ear. He leaves.*

REGGIE. Erm that's fine, mate, just make sure you're by yourself is that crystal clear?

REGGIE *leaves.*

Scene Seven

Moments later, at the wall. REGGIE *paces. Anxiety seeps out of his skin. He is very uneasy. He has a brown sack clutched under his arm.* OBI *arrives, even more anxious and edgy than* REGGIE.

REGGIE. You're late! I was gonna leave.

OBI. Have you got it?

> REGGIE *clinically combs the area, making sure nobody is around.*

> (*Impatiently.*) Have you got it, Reggie?

REGGIE. Yes.

> REGGIE *unzips the sack.*

OBI. I'm not gonna kill him. I just wanna scare him. I wouldn't kill him.

> After this we're gonna get you some help, Reggie. We'll go down to the hospital and you could start a programme or something. Get you cleaned up for good. After that you could get a job and be whatever you wanna be, Reg. It's not too late to turn things back around. You're not expected to deal with this all on your own.

> OBI*'s phone rings.*

REGGIE. Hurry up.

The sky lets out a cry of thunder. A storm breaks.

OBI. Chelsea! Look don't worry about me, I'll call you back… hello… hello? Cain, is that you?! What? Don't talk me to death, do something – do something… you *know* where I am! I'm at the estate wall! COME! I'm here now, bruv, and I don't see you! What? *Ah don't believe youuuu!* Touch Chelsea and see what happens to you, bruv, touch her and see what happens… what? DON'T FINK I DON'T KNOW THEY ATE YOU ALIVE IN THERE! COME! I'M THERE NOW, BRUV!

He drops the phone.

Shit! He's got her phone.

REGGIE (*impatiently*). Have you got the money?

   OBI *pulls out the cash and shows* REGGIE. *It's the same money that* CAIN *gave to him.*

OBI. Let me see it, Reggie. (Fuck.) Hold it out to me.

   REGGIE *significantly steps back from* OBI.

   He pulls an object out of the sack, it's wrapped in a brown cloth.

   Slowly he begins to unwrap it but then quickly covers it back up.

   What you doing?

REGGIE. Ay what say we do this in the alley just there – we don't want everybody to see.

   OBI *wants to get this transaction over and done with. He goes ahead, down the alley, off-stage.* REGGIE *follows behind, the bag in his hand. Then from offstage, we hear –*

   BANG!

   Long beat.

   BANG!

   REGGIE *runs back on stage, scattering away. Stuffing the gun back into the bag. A fist full of cash. His hands are trembling. He drops some. The money has blood on it. He picks it up. Scurries away.*

   Black.

Scene Eight

At the wall. Against the estate wall are roses, OBI*'s Year 7 picture and* OBI*'s book.*

Enter MYLES.

He takes a deep breath.

MYLES (*to us*). Day three-six-six on *Camera-Phone Diaries: Council Estate of Mind.*

Today's a very special day, we're back at my old estate.

A year ago I started these recordings, not really knowing what I wanted to do with them or what they meant even, but it all began right here. Many days spent at this wall.

Today, we pay our respects to my boy Obi, who you'll remember from volume one. Obi One-Yendu tragically died here a year ago today. Rest in peace. Obi One inspired me to be me, he was the one who inspired me to start these documentaries, he was a poet, he participated in moving forward and upwards and just hanging around him was enough to make me wanna do the same – Predominantly, after he left us.

So I just wanna say, much obliged to you, Obi, my hat goes off, we miss you.

Pause.

This is exactly what we need to open our eyes to – what's gwarnin around us. No one will benefit from closing his or her eyes to knives and cables cutting into faces and mouths of our young and old, or from bullets piercing our beloved Obi whose only sin was his quest for freedom – no one.

I know you're still around. I can feel you, b.

So keep the letters coming in, if there's a problem in your estate or in your ends, we wanna talk about it.

Big Myles, signing out.

If you can't be good, be careful.

MYLES *goes to sit at the wall. He picks up* OBI*'s picture, he looks at it. He selects a poem from* OBI*'s book, he reads to himself.*

OBI*'s spirit enters, wearing a Royal Navy uniform. He stands there, proud.*

Fade to black.

End of play.

A Nick Hern Book

Little Baby Jesus and *Estate Walls* first published in Great Britain in 2019 as a paperback original by Nick Hern Books Limited, The Glasshouse, 49a Goldhawk Road, London W12 8QP, in association with the Orange Tree Theatre, Richmond

Little Baby Jesus first published as a single edition in 2011

Cover image: © shutterstock.com

Designed and typeset by Nick Hern Books, London
Printed in the UK by Mimeo Ltd, Huntingdon, Cambridgeshire PE29 6XX

A CIP catalogue record for this book is available from the British Library

ISBN 978 1 84842 919 2

www.nickhernbooks.co.uk

facebook.com/nickhernbooks

twitter.com/nickhernbooks